161 433619 9

D0352952

One week loan
Benthyciad un wythnos

Please return on or before the due date to avoid overdue charges
*A wnewch chi ddychwelyd ar neu cyn y dyddiad a nodir ar eich llyfr os
gwelwch yn dda, er mwyn osgoi taliadau*

✓ 14/12/06 AS	WITHDRAWN

http://library.cardiff.ac.uk
http://llyfrgell.caerdydd.ac.uk

174.9687
M

First Published 2006
The Institute of Chartered Accountants of Scotland

© 2006
ISBN 1 904574-18-1

This book is published for the Research Committee of
The Institute of Chartered Accountants of Scotland.
The views expressed in this report are those of the author
and do not necessarily represent the views of
the Council of the Institute or the Research Committee.

No responsibility for loss occasioned to any person acting
or refraining from action as a result of any material
in this publication can be accepted by the author or publisher.

All rights reserved. No part of this publication may be
reproduced, stored in a retrieval system, or transmitted, in
any form or by any means, electronic, mechanical, photocopy,
recording or otherwise, without prior permission of the publisher.

CARDIFF UNIVERSITY
★ 3 0 NOV 2006 ★
PRIFYSGOL CAERDYDD

Printed and bound in Great Britain
by T J International Ltd

Contents

FOREWORD

In October 2004 the Research Committee of ICAS published *Taking Ethics to Heart*, an investigation into the ethical standing of accountants. It examined a number of remedies to ensure that appropriate mechanisms were in place to ensure 'good' decision making.

This literature review is the second in a series of three commissioned literature reviews associated with *Taking Ethics to Heart*. This review is published at a time when the ethical standing of accountants in the eyes of the general public continues to be an issue for the profession and the corporate world at large and when regulatory and professional bodies continue to seek solutions to these problems.

The literature review considers *Ethics and the Individual Professional Accountant* and analyses the literature on the changing nature of individual professional ethics.

Chapter one of the report reviews the ethical nature of individuals and concludes that the ethical tendencies of individual accounting students and practising accountants are not as developed as might be expected. A model is then developed to highlight the individual, contextual and issue related factors which play a role in the way that accountants experience and respond to ethical issues.

The next chapter explores the literature on the nature of professionalism. This explores the idea that professionalism might influence the way an accountant identifies, experiences and responds to ethical dilemmas and looks at the characteristics traditionally associated with the idea of professionalism. The author concludes that while the accounting profession appears to possess these characteristics they seem to lack substance.

Chapter three then explores six broad historical shifts which may have influenced individual accountants' perceptions of what it means to be a professional.

In the final chapter the report summarises the findings of the literature review and then considers some of the more practical recommendations for progressing the ethical tendencies of individual accountants. The author recognises that this is a complex issue and that isolated reforms may have a harmful impact on professional identity. The most pertinent recommendations relate to education and *Taking Ethics to Heart* contributes significantly to this debate. The author also identifies three further emerging issues and recommendations: a collaborative approach by the major professions to ethics education; Service Based Learning programmes, which facilitates student involvement in local community activities; and the provision of Pro-Bono work by accounting professionals.

In addition the author identifies the following as areas for future research: investigation into practitioners' views of professionalism; accounting knowledge and how this relates to professionals' claims to serve the public interest; civic education and how notions of the public interest may be incorporated into professional education; and how individuals' perceptions of accounting and what it means to be a professional accountant are developed before attendance at university.

The Research Committee of The Institute of Chartered Accountants of Scotland, through the auspices of the Scottish Chartered Accountants Trust for Education, has been happy to sponsor this project and is pleased that the literature review is becoming available at a time when the subject matter is so topical and the profession's response is critical. The Committee recognises that the views expressed do not necessarily represent those of ICAS itself, but hopes that this project will contribute to the current debate on ethics and professionalism.

David Spence
Convener,
Research Committee

May 2006

Acknowledgements

Thanks to Louise Brown for help with the literature review. Thanks also to the ICAS Research Committee and especially Christine Helliar, for their insightful comments and helpful guidance. Finally, special thanks to Steve Walker for his guidance on the historical development of the profession; to Aileen Pierce; and to Isobel Webber for her expert administration.

EXECUTIVE SUMMARY

This report is part of a broader process of ethical reflection and review being undertaken by The Institute of Chartered Accountants of Scotland. As is the case with many individuals, the Institute's pause for reflection may be related both to its maturation and the fact that over the past few years the accounting profession has gone through a period of intense crisis. It is therefore not insignificant that the project coincides with the Institute's 150th Anniversary or that it comes in the wake of the Enron, WorldCom and Parmalat debacles (see ICAS, 2004; Morrison, 2004).

To mark the Institute's 150th Anniversary and, no doubt, as part of the profession's process of post-Enron self-examination, The Institute of Chartered Accountants of Scotland commissioned a tripartite series of reviews that aim to explore professional ethics in some detail (see Lovell, 2005; Pierce, 2006). This series of reviews begins to explore the complexity of professional ethics by bringing together disparate but related discussions from a broad range of accounting, moral philosophy and psychology literatures. Alan Lovell's report collates the literature on 'ethics in business' in general and Aileen Pierce's review focuses on the insights that the literature provides into ethics and professional accounting firms. This report focuses on the literature on 'ethics and the individual professional accountant'.

Taken together, these reports (along with ICAS, 2004) provide a basis for beginning to explore the complex ethical challenges facing the profession as it heads into the 21st Century.

This report reviews the literature on 'ethics and the individual professional accountant'. The study draws on a broad range of literature in an attempt to begin to model the complexity of individual ethical behaviour with a view to highlighting the types of issues that the Institute may need to consider if it is to engage with individual professional ethical development in a meaningful way. The report discusses the following issues:

1. The ethical predisposition of accountants in particular.

2. The nature of the ethical individual.

3. The structure of the ethical issues that individuals face.

4. The characteristics of professions and professionalism.

5. Changes in both the perception and experience of professionalism.

6. How the profession might begin to engage with changing conceptualisations of professionalism.

7. Experience within the other professions.

8. Findings from other countries.

The new millennium has not started well for accountants. The collapse of Enron, and the ignominious fall of the accounting institution Andersens, followed by WorldCom then Parmalat, has thrown the profession into crisis … again! Accountants are no strangers to scandal. Since its inception 150 years ago, the profession has consistently experienced periods of crisis (see Edwards, 2001), from the Royal Mail scandal in the 1930s (Mitchell and Sikka, 1993) to allegations of money laundering in the 1990s (Mitchell, Sikka and Wilmott, 1998). So the question of professional ethics has come to the fore again.

But what is the question? Clearly, professional ethics encompasses an individual's response to ethical dilemmas. Was David Duncan, the partner responsible for the Enron audit, wrong to shred audit working papers? Certainly there is a need to understand how individuals experience ethical dilemmas within specific circumstances and the factors that influence their response. There is also a need to question what individual moral development means and how the profession can help accountants, faced with complex ethical dilemmas in practice, to make the right decisions. But the question of individual professional ethics is broader than this. It involves the function of accounting within the political and economic system. Arthur Wood of the Securities and Exchange Commission once commented, in relation to an earlier accounting crisis, that:

> ... *the cause of this crisis is the fact that investors and depositors are losing faith in the ability of the accounting profession to perform the job that has historically been its unique function: assuring the integrity of financial information on which our capitalistic society depends.* (P Armstrong, 1987).

The professional ethics of individual accountants is linked to the functioning of the capital market system. The accounting profession currently gains its legitimacy from its ability to perform this particular function (Hooks, 1991) and this may, in turn, explain the level of state interest in the accounting profession post Enron (See for example, Fearnley and Beattie, 2004).

This crisis[1], like previous debacles (for example Polly Peck, Coloroll and Sound Diffusion) is therefore socio-political in its nature and hints at a broader systemic failing (See for example Puxty, 1997 and McKernan and O'Donnell, 1997).

Yet Enron *et al.* pushes the professional ethics debate into new territory. It is different from previous crises in detail. Much of the analysis, for example, has focused on the technical complexities of accounting for complicated financial transactions. The concern is that the concepts and categories of conventional accounting practice are now outmoded and struggling to cope with contemporary business practice. However, more significantly, the socio-economic context of the Enron debacle also differs from previous cases. Yes, the scandal occurred in a period when international capital markets were distinctly bearish and had been for some time, but more importantly, it happened in a period of changing social attitudes towards both business and the professions. It occurred within a milieu of increased questioning of the role of business in society and post-modern scepticism regarding the authority and function of the professions (Hauptman and Hill, 1991; Dillard and Yuthas, 2002).

Enron, therefore, presents a significant challenge to the profession. However, the challenge comes not only in the need to understand the nature of the specific ethical dilemmas individual accountants face, and how the profession can help its members to respond to them in an appropriate way, but it also presents a challenge to the routine functioning of accounting within society. It represents an opportunity for the profession to critically engage with changing public expectations in relation to the civic functioning of the professions.

The aim of this particular study is to critically analyse and synthesise the literature on the changing nature of individual professional ethics. The report takes its structure from the remit given for the study: '*ethics and the individual professional accountant*', and is split into four main chapters. Following some brief comments on the method employed, the report initially focuses on the ethical nature of individuals and the structure of ethical issues. This section provides the context for considering how individuals may experience and respond to ethical issues in practice. Chapter two extends the discussion by focusing on the characteristics of professionalism. The purpose of this chapter is twofold. Firstly, one would imagine that within the sphere of accounting, the idea of professionalism might influence the way an accountant identifies, experiences and responds to ethical dilemmas. However, this chapter also attempts to begin to expand the discussion of professional ethics into the arena of public expectations, civic responsibilities and the public interest in general, if indeed, this is what being a professional is about. The penultimate chapter considers whether the notion of professionalism has changed over time and the report concludes by exploring some of the suggested responses to the crisis within the literature. Some suggestions for further research are also provided.

The research discussed in chapters one to four is used to develop a framework for beginning to think about the complexity of the ethics of individual professional accountants.

Given that this study is part of a broader ethics project, the report attempts to engage with the other reviews in the series and also the ICAS Research Committee's perspective on these issues as discussed in its report *Taking Ethics to Heart*. It is perhaps in this potential for open dialogue and debate, created, in part, by the collapse of Enron that the greatest opportunity for substantive change is found.

ENDNOTE:

---

[1] This study employs Puxty's (1997) definition of crisis as, 'a state reached by a system such that to continue its operation in the same way beyond that point becomes unfeasible: structural changes must be made, otherwise the system will fail generally as a result of imminent contradictory forces acting upon it'.

CHAPTER ONE

ETHICS AND THE INDIVIDUAL

Introduction

The method employed in this study was determined by the project remit. The specific aim of the study was to synthesise the literature that may provide useful insights for understanding the changing ways in which individual professional accountants experience ethical issues. The process of determining which literatures are relevant to the topic is, however, somewhat problematic and it is, therefore, important to highlight the limitations of the study at the outset.

While the review made use of broad database search engines, the review primarily focused on the discussion of professions within the accounting and business ethics literature. A list of the journals specifically reviewed is provided in appendix one. The review drew on some of the psychology literature and also some of the broader professional literature, specifically, law, medicine and engineering.

The review is, therefore, limited in its scope and most probably does not capture the full complexity of the issue. This is relevant and should caution against both the tendency to over-simplify professional ethics and the propensity to rush into simplistic and inadequate responses to the apparent failings within the profession.

Three distinct themes were identified within the literature in relation to ethics and the individual (Genz, 1997). These themes, along with their associated issues are as follows:

Empirical/Descriptive perspectives on ethics and the individual

This section covers:
- Empirical evidence relating to the behaviour of accountants;
- Moral development models;
- Individual attributes and ethical behaviour: the effect of gender and age;
- Ethics and the embedded accountant;
- Ethics and the roles accountants play;
- Moral intensity; and
- Moral framing.

Normative perspectives on ethics and individual behaviour

This section covers:
- Deontological ethics;
- Teleological ethics;
- Virtue-based approaches to individual action; and
- Reason and moral sense theory.

Analytical perspectives on ethics and the individual

This section covers:
- The Individual as the basis of moral reflection;
- The rights and duties of individuals; and
- Post-structural perspectives on individual ethics.

Insights from each of these three different perspectives will be used to begin to develop a framework for thinking about the ethics of the individual in general.

The nature of individual, professional and ethical predispositions is undoubtedly complex. Such is the paucity of ethical reflection and analysis within the accounting profession, that at this stage, the aim is simply to identify the kinds of issues that need to be considered to begin to seriously engage with professional ethics. This opening section draws on insights from the broader business ethics and moral philosophy literature to begin to develop a framework for thinking about the ethics of individual accountants. It aims to identity some of the key factors involved in understanding individual ethics and provides the context for exploring the ethics of professionalism in particular, in the following section.

The broader panoply of business ethics and moral philosophy literature can be split into three broad but distinct perspectives: Empirical, Normative and Analytical perspectives (Grenz, 1997). Insights from each of these three different perspectives will be used to begin to develop a framework for thinking about the ethics of the individual in general.

The descriptive moral philosophy literature seems like an obvious place to begin this review, as the subject invokes a series of quite rudimentary, empirical questions: How do accountants behave in practice? Are they generally ethical or unethical? What factors influence their ethical predispositions? Do accountants respond to ethical dilemmas in a different way as professional accountants than they would if they experienced the same dilemmas in some other capacity? And, what does ethical development mean, how can it be said that one accountant is more or less ethically developed than another? The first sub-section draws on the extensive empirical literature to provide some insights into these and other questions.

Western, secular reflection on ethics and the individual can be traced back to Socrates and his question, 'How ought I to behave?' The second section provides some brief insights into this normative debate on how individuals should act. Two traditional responses to this question are briefly described, one based on deduced principles, the other, on virtue theory. This brief outline poses more fundamental questions in relation to the ethics of individual accountants. This literature provides some insights into how accountants are taught, both explicitly and implicitly, what constitutes appropriate moral behaviour. However, it also highlights that this particular approach is only one of a number of alternatives to resolving ethical issues. There is also a brief introduction to a related debate on the bases upon which individual ethical decisions should be made. Within the literature there is a significant debate between those who view 'reason' as an appropriate basis for responding to all ethical dilemmas and others who suggest that some kind of 'moral empathy' is required.

The third section explores ethics and the individual from an analytical perspective. The objective of this section is to summarise the literature on the basis and nature of ethics as it relates to individuals. The section commences by exploring the work of Jean-Jacques Rousseau. Rousseau was not so much concerned with specific individual action, as with the more fundamental question of why an individual should behave in an ethical way. This review is followed by a brief discussion of the rights and duties of individuals. The section concludes by exploring the radically different orientation provided by post-structuralist perspectives on individual ethical behaviour. This discussion provides insights into a number of broader political economic questions in relation to individual professional ethics. Firstly, what individual rights does accounting support? And in what sense can the normal practice of individual accountants be ethically justified? (see Figure 1.1).

Figure 1.1: A Professional Ethics Model

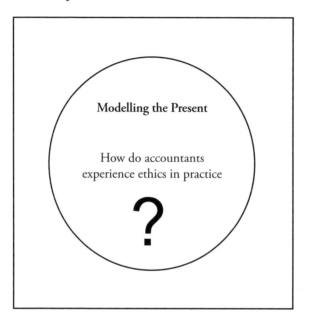

Empirical evidence relating to the behaviour of accountants

The first section commences by reviewing the extensive empirical literature that seeks to describe how accountants and individuals behave in practice.

Within the accounting literature, many academics have expressed concern over the ethical predispositions of both accounting students (Gray *et al.* 1994; Lehman, 1988) and accounting practitioners (Denham, 1991; Stanga and Turpen, 1991; Beets and Killough, 1990; Schlachter, 1990; Ponemon, 1990; 1992).

A significant number of studies indicate that accountants seem to exhibit lower levels of moral reasoning than other professional groups (Eynon *et al.* 1997). Studies by M B Armstrong (1987) and Ponemon

(1992) for example, suggest that accountants' moral maturity is lagging behind that of other professional groups.

Within the literature, there is considerable debate as to the contribution of accounting and business education to this worrying observation. In particular, the literature questions the extent to which accounting education impairs accountants' ethical development (Gray *et al.* 1994). Jeffrey (1993) (see also Arlow, 1991) contends that the ethical development of accounting students is higher than their college peers. Davis and Welton (1991) also found an improvement in accounting students' ethical tendencies over the course of their degree programmes, but they attributed this development to their general maturation rather than to any specific ethical training that they received. By contrast, Lane and Shaupp (1989), Mayer (1988), McCabe *et al.* (1991) and Gray *et al.* (1994) all suggest that business and accounting education has a negative effect on students' ethical proclivities. For example, Mayer (1988) found that business students do not recognise the broader social responsibility issues associated with professionalism. Borkowski and Ugras (1992) hint that this immaturity in ethical awareness may be related to an apparent shift in ethical orientation from a justice-based perspective towards a utilitarian viewpoint.

Loeb (1991) (see also Rosen & Caplan, 1990; Macklin 1980) goes as far as to suggest that students have been indoctrinated into believing simply that, 'the role of business in society is to produce goods and services at a profit' (McCabe *et al.* 1991) and that ethics and social responsibility are unimportant considerations in corporate decision making unless they have a direct impact on production or profits (Friedman, 1970, in Jensen and Wygart, 1990). Merritt (1991) (see also Hawkins & Cocanougher, 1972) implies that the propagation of ideas like this have 'tainted students by making them mercenary in their approach to their craft'. He contends that there is a clear indication that business degrees are associated with lower ethical standards[1] and he concludes that, 'business schools have not done an adequate job of preparing students to respond ethically to the complex issues that arise in the work environment'. However, the profession is also to blame for not insisting that ethics forms a greater part of the broader professional curriculum. Hauptman and Hill (1991), somewhat scathingly conclude that the professions are operating as 'amoral economic pressure groups immune from ethical concerns', and as a consequence, public opinion is becoming increasingly characterised by the same level of cynicism.

Taken together, the literature presents the somewhat disturbing possibility that conventional accounting education has a negative impact on students' ethical predispositions (Arlow 1991). Fleming (1996), for example, concludes that 'the tendency of the evidence is to suggest, if anything, that accountants either occupy the middle ground or lean towards an amoral ethical position'. ICAS's (2004) investigation of ICAS members is not inconsistent with this conclusion.

In terms of the ethics of the individual professional, therefore, the literature suggests that both qualified accountants and accounting students view the everyday practice of accounting as an amoral activity and that accounting education may be a contributing factor in the inculcation of such pre-dispositions. Given the role accounting plays in implementing socio-economic ideology, whether in a free-market, centralised or mixed economy, this is a worrying conclusion. In the UK, for example, accounting information contributes to the functioning of the capital market and, as such, helps to facilitate the system of distributional justice upon which this system is based.

However, while there seems to be some concern within the literature over the ethical maturity of accountants there appears to be similar unease within other professional literatures. Concern over professional ethics is widely discussed within the engineering literature[2] (Kucner, 1993; Koehn, 1991). Koehn (1991), Herkert and Viscomi (1991), and Florman (1987) all address the problem of the unethical behaviour of engineers. Porter (1993) compares the behaviour of some professional engineering societies with their stated expectations for the behaviour of their members and finds a double standard. He suggests that this inconsistency has contributed towards a poor public profile for the engineering profession (Bruneau, 1994; 1993), an observation that resonates within the accounting literature. Bruneau (1994, see also Kucner, 1993) observes that 'displays of professional dissatisfaction in the trade literature have increased with alarming frequency ... to such an extent that the casual reader may think that the profession is terminally ill'. The engineering profession is obviously not indifferent to its public perception and the recognition of these problems has invoked calls for action (Martin and Schinzinger, 1989; Vann, 1992). There have been calls to include ethics in professional exams (Koehn 1992) and calls for companies to establish professional ethics education training programmes for their employees[3](Kucner, 1993, see also Herkert and Viscomi, 1991; Koehn, 1991; Koehn, 1992). Kucner (1993, see also Wilcox 1983; Holliday, 1994; Anderson, 1994) explains that the reason why the profession is concerned about the public's perception is because of the potentially adverse effect that unethical behaviour can have on the profession's credibility and legitimacy.

Concern over individual professional ethics seems to be quite different in the medical literature. Williamson (1996) (see also Myser *et al.* 1995) argues that 'medicine is fundamentally an ethical pursuit'. He implies that medical students are the most intelligent of university students and therefore, the most ethical! Indeed, within the medical literature it is generally contended that medical students enter their courses with high moral dispositions (Hafferty and Franks, 1994). Williamson (1996) for example suggests that, 'unlike other students, every medical student enters university an idealist with the intention of behaving in an overtly ethical fashion'. In a similar vein, Gillon (1996) explains that medical ethics education is not intended to 'improve the moral character of student doctors, but rather to provide those of sound moral character, who have been selected to become medical students, with the intellectual tools and interactional skills to give their moral character its best expression'.

However, Green *et al.* (1995) have described how this idealistic attitude of student doctors fails to survive as they proceed through their medical education. They express particular concern at evidence that suggests that medical students' ethical sensitivity diminishes during the course of their training. Similarly, Miles *et al.* (1989) discuss growing concerns over the personal attributes and declining 'humanistic sensitivity,' of doctors. Miles *et al.* (1989) place the blame for this 'dehumanisation' on an 'overly scientised' trend in pre-medical education. They also argue that the structure of the medical degree syllabus is partially responsible for increased cynicism amongst medical students. Similarly, Hafferty and Franks (1994), (see also Parker, 1995) discuss the way ethics is marginalised in the culture of medicine because emphasis is placed on the transmission of technical skills and knowledge. Hafferty and Franks (1994) conclude that the professional culture of medics has become 'ethically compromised'. This concern over the technical nature of medical education resonates with debates within the accounting literature.

A review of the legal education journals also reveals a considerable level of concern over the ethical predispositions of lawyers. Lieberman (1979); Kronman (1993); Luban (1983); Smith (1990); and Webb (1996) have all expressed concern at the unethical behaviour of lawyers[4]. Smith (1990) for example, contends that 'lawyers roles expose them to great risk of moral wrongdoing' and is also concerned that being a lawyer 'inevitably corrupts lawyer's characters'. In a similar vein, Wasserstrom (1984) suggests that the lawyers world is 'a simplified moral world'. He says, 'often it is an amoral world; and more than occasionally perhaps, an overtly immoral one'. The ethical status of the legal profession in the UK has also been the subject of major institutional scrutiny. The Lord Chancellor's Advisory Committee's, the Advisory Committee on Legal Education and Conduct, 'First Report', for example, has addressed the ethical problems of the legal profession (Webb 1996). Thus, as with the medical and engineering professions, there is considerable concern within the literature over the ethics of lawyers and it is expected that concern over ethics will continue to grow (Moliterno 1996).

There appears, therefore, to be a significant level of concern across many of the traditional professions over the ethical characteristics of their members. It would seem that the concern over the ethics of individual professional accountants is not an isolated case but is also mirrored across the other main professions. This hints at a broader crisis in professionalism which may be related to a perceptible shift in social attitudes towards the professions.

Moral development models

A considerable number of the comparative studies discussed above draw on the work of Lawrence Kohlberg and his model of Cognitive Moral Development (see Ponemon, 1990). Kohlberg's model is routinely used to gauge an individual's moral maturity (Reiter, 1996) based on their responses to a series of hypothetical dilemmas. Most of the conventional studies in the accounting literature use Rest's Defining Issues Test to collect data on individual predispositions and this is subsequently analysed using Kohlberg's model (Bay, 2002). The model itself consists of six discrete predispositions (see figure 1.2.)

Figure 1.2: Kohlberg's Model of Cognitive Moral Development

Levels	Stages	Disposition
3. Post-Conventional	6	Based on universal moral principles.
	5	Impartial, with a concern for everyone's interests
2. Conventional	4	Informed by society's laws
	3	Conforming to group norms
1. Pre-Conventional	2	Self interest is the primary motivation
	1	Avoid punishment

Cognitive Moral Development has been applied to accounting students, accounting practitioners at various stages in their careers (Ponemon, 1990), students studying different disciplines and practitioners from different professions. This model has also been used in comparisons of ethics in different national cultures (Kracher *et al.* 2002) and the impact of organisational culture on individual ethical behaviour (Forte, 2004). Other studies have applied Cognitive Moral Development to organisations, as opposed to individuals, in an attempt to explore whether it is possible to position groups at different stages in Kohlberg's model.

However, while this model is quite prominent within the literature, there is a growing body of work that critiques Kohlberg's model. To begin with, there is some debate as to whether a different level of moral reasoning necessarily results in different forms of behaviour (Reiter, 1996). However, at a more fundamental level, Reiter (1996) critiques the model itself. She contrasts Kohlberg's conceptualisation of moral development with that of Carol Gilligan. Reiter (1996) suggests that while Kohlberg conceptualises progress in moral thinking in terms of increased abstraction and autonomy, Gilligan's 'ethics of care' presents a more embedded and empathic view of ethical development. Gilligan was particularly concerned that Kohlberg's model had been developed primarily from studies of male volunteers. However, Reiter (1996) presents Gilligan's contrasting model (see figure 1.3), not as a replacement for Cognitive Moral Development but rather as a complementary perspective that should be combined with Kohlberg's model.

Figure 1.3: Gilligan's Hierarchy of Moral Development

Third Focus	Dynamic inter-relationship between the self and others.
Transition: Questioning of logic of inequality between the needs of others and one's self	
Second Focus	Care for dependent others, involving self sacrifice
Transition: Focus on self seen as unacceptably selfish	
First Focus	Caring for one's self and ensuring survival

Both Gilligan's and Kohlberg's work are pertinent for exploring individual professional ethics and beginning to develop a framework for thinking about professional ethics (see figure 1.4). Their work encourages reflection on how to conceptualise the moral development of the individual accountant. However, both models provide different ways of thinking about the kinds of attributes that might characterise ethical maturity and show that moral development is both complex and contested.

There are also obvious educational implications depending on the type of model espoused. Reiter (1996) suggests that the majority of ethics education within accounting is focused on a case-study approach, underpinned by the Kohlberg model. Developing an ethics of care, as

Reiter points out, requires a significantly different form of educational practice (McPhail, 2001).

Figure 1.4: Modelling Professional Ethics: Empirical Perspectives

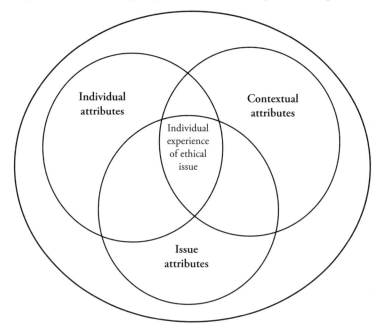

Individual attributes	Issue attributes	Contextual attributes
• Moral maturity	• Nature of Consequences	• Categorisation
• Age	• Social Consensus	• Organisation
• Gender	• Possibility of Effect	• Linguistic framing
• Nationality	• Temporal immediacy	• Place
	• Proximity	
	• Concentration of effect.	

Individual attributes and ethical behaviour: The effect of age and gender

Kohlberg's model is also used within the literature to explore the impact of gender and age on individual ethical tendencies (Whipple and Swords, 1992). While Stanga and Turpen's (1991) work does not support the existence of gender differences, Arlow (1991), Miesing and Preble (1985) and Borkowski and Ugras (1992) contend that females are more ethical than males. David *et al.* (1994) also suggest that women have different kinds of attitudes towards ethics and codes of ethics.

While female accountants' experiences of professionalism may differ from those of their male counterparts, this literature also examines gender in a broader sense referring to more general masculine and feminine personality traits as opposed to biological gender. There is some evidence to suggest that accounting education promotes the development of masculine character traits within students and that this may, in turn, have an impact on the way accountants as a group conceptualise and respond to ethical dilemmas (Bebbington *et al.* 1997).

Cognitive moral development research has also provided overwhelming evidence that moral reasoning is affected by age (Trevino, 1992; Rest, 1983; Serwenek, 1992). (See figure 1.4). It would appear that individual characteristics generally have quite a significant influence on ethical tendencies.

Ethics and the embedded accountant

While this review focuses on the ethics of the individual it is important to highlight the complexity of extracting individual accountants from the structures within which they are embedded. Fogarty (1995) for example, contends that the tendency to separate individual accountants from their context has been one of the limitations of accounting and business ethics research. He contends that this focus on individual ethical actions is inconsistent with the emphasis within the sociological literature on the importance of the complex socio-economic relationships within which the individual is embedded. Two issues discussed within the literature are worthy of brief mention: firstly cultural issues and secondly organisational factors.

Culture

There is a considerable discussion within the literature on the influence of culture on the ethical predispositions of individuals and whether different national value systems affect an individual's understanding of ethical behaviour (Spranger, 1928, in Karnes *et al.* 1990). Jakubowski *et al.* (2002) suggest that national differences are reflected in the ethical codes of accountants across different countries and Karnes *et al.* (1990) contend that accountants of different nationalities have disparate perceptions of what is, and is not, ethical. Cohen *et al.* (1992) draw on Hofstede's cultural studies to argue that there are international differences in ethical values that could impede the effectiveness of the International Federation of Accountants (IFAC) *Guidelines on ethics for professional accountants.* IFAC states that:

> *Differing cultures and levels of economic development are likely to cause professionals in many countries to find some part of international guidelines irrelevant to their needs, and even for some, antithetical to the social and economic environment in which they work.*

However, Lysonski and Gaidis (1991) found that students' responses to ethical dilemmas are similar across cultures and Whipple and Swords (1992) similarly suggest that demographic factors do not influence ethical proclivities.

Organisations and groups of individuals

The literature also stresses that any attempt to understand the ethical tendencies of individual accountants must recognise that they are embedded within organisations. The ethics of accounting firms is the subject of Aileen Pierce's report and is not discussed in detail here. However, two points are briefly mentioned in passing: 'group think' and 'organisational culture'.

Individual accountants are embedded within at least two primary organisational settings, both of which may influence individual ethical tendencies: the profession and the firm, or company. While at one level, an organisation is, in part, a grouping of individuals, the literature suggests that individuals' ethical tendency may change when they become part of a crowd or more formal grouping (Hauptman and Hill, 1991). Sims (1992) labels this phenomenon 'group think'.

Douglas *et al.* (2001, see also Schlachter 1990) imply that ethical predispositions are also affected by organisational culture. Indeed, a number of studies have shown that personal values often have little impact on ethical decisions in business or within organisational contexts (Shafer *et al.* 2001, see also Akaah and Lund, 1994; Finegan, 1994, in Shafer *et al*, 2001). Grey (1998) implies that the organisational settings where work takes place are emotion free and that this can have a significant impact on the way individuals identify and resolve ethical dilemmas. Individual ethics also often change depending upon the position and level that an individual occupies within an organisation. Ponemon (1990) finds that ethical reasoning capacity increases in staff at supervisory levels but then decreases amongst managers and partners (see also Trevino 1992, in Reiter 1996). He suggests a number of possibilities for his findings, including conflicting social influences at different hierarchical levels and the possibility of self-selection processes at work. Tyson's (1990) work suggests that individuals generally think they are more ethical than their peers and co-workers.

To appreciate the complex inter-relationship between individual ethical tendencies and the national and organisational contexts within which individuals are embedded, this report and Aileen Pierce's review should be viewed as inter-related. An understanding of the ethics of individual accountants requires an understanding of the ethics of professional accounting firms.

Ethics and the roles accountants play

The complex inter-relationship between individual predispositions and social structures has, more recently, drawn on the findings in the social psychology literature. As a consequence, some studies focus on whether individual accountants subscribe to different ethical values within different parts of their lives, or whether individuals' conceptualisation of ethical issues differ depending on the context within which they are experienced. This possibility is also discussed in Lovell's (2005) discussion of 'ethical schizophrenia'.

The study of the way that information is encoded in memory is a central issue in both learning theory and cognitive psychology (Tajfel and Fraser, 1990) and has been conceptualised using the notion of categorisation (Tajfel and Fraser, 1990; Hewstone *et al.* 1993; Campbell, 1963, in Tajfel and Fraser 1990; Shaw and Wright, 1967; Cole and Scribner, 1974). According to learning theory, the process of categorisation involves learning to ascribe specific properties to particular groups of objects (Stahlberg and Frey, 1988, in Tajfel and Fraser, 1990). Learning theorists suggest that the resulting connections are organised and stored in cognitive memory structures called schema[5] (Markus 1977; Fiske and Taylor 1984; Schwarz 1985, in Hewstone *et al.* 1993; Taylor and Corcker, 1981; Choo 1989). These schema are assumed to direct attention to relevant information and guide its interpretation and evaluation. Categorisations are thus seen to play a primary role in an individual's understanding of the world and identifying appropriate ways of behaving within it (see Fogarty, 1992).

Within the cognitive psychology literature, the notion of *scripts* has been developed to reflect the function that sequences of actions play in forming the basis of different behavioural roles, for example, visiting a doctor, going to the supermarket, or more pertinently, performing an audit. It is argued that scriptal knowledge structures[6] retain knowledge of expected sequences of behaviours, actions, and events.

If becoming an accountant is associated with the acquisition of a related 'accountant' cognitive script, then this has obvious implications for the way accountants might experience ethical issues as accountants. However, this research also hints at a more interesting possibility. It maybe that accountants respond to similar ethical issues in different ways, depending on the cognitive context within which they are experienced. A study by Weber (1990), for example, finds that managers' moral reasoning levels are lower in work-related decision situations compared to non-work related dilemmas. Trevino (1992) similarly suggests that different values, norms and behaviours are associated with different 'life domains'.

From the studies reviewed it would appear that both individual attributes and contextual characteristics influence individual ethics. However, the literature also suggests that the structure and attributes of ethical issues themselves can have a significant impact on the way individuals conceptualise and respond to specific dilemmas. This section of the report introduces various attempts within the literature to model the structure of ethical issues (see figure 1.4).

A significant body of work within the business ethics literature focuses on situational ethics. The main premise of this model is that both the nature of ethical issues, and individuals' responses to them, will be influenced by the context within which the issue is encountered. Although not explicitly connected within the literature, there is an obvious link between situational ethics and the concept of categorisation discussed above. The literature discusses two main types of situational influences: issue-related elements and context-related elements. Some of the context specific issues like age, gender and organisational setting discussed above have been shown to have a significant impact on the way individuals construe their ethical obligations and respond to ethical issues. However, this body of research recognises that the nature of ethical issues themselves is also important in understanding an individual's ethical predisposition towards them. The following sub-sections focus specifically on two issue-related elements: moral intensity and moral framing.

Moral intensity

Jones (1991) suggests that the moral intensity of an issue is influenced by six factors:

(i) The nature of the consequences;

(ii) The social consensus;

(iii) The possibility of effect;

(iv) Temporal immediacy;

(v) Proximity; and

(vi) The concentration of effect.

The nature of the consequences relates to the magnitude of the outcome of ones actions. Social consensus refers to the general social attitude towards the particular issue. The possibility of effect is to do with the probability that a particular set of consequences will ensue from an individual's action. Temporal immediacy relates to the speed with which the consequences are likely to come into effect, whereas proximity refers to the nearness to individuals who are likely to be affected by ones actions. The final element relates to the number of people likely to be affected by a particular action. The elements of this model are quite readily applicable to accounting and business decisions. For example, it might be easier to advocate a particular investment project if any potentially negative impacts are both uncertain and unlikely to materialise for many years. While it may be difficult to isolate the specific impact of any one of these factors, the inter-relationship between them will have a significant influence on the way an individual will engage with a particular ethical issue (see figure 1.4).

Moral framing

The associated issue of moral framing suggests that individuals respond to ethical dilemmas in different ways depending on the framework within which they are experienced. Two strands of research elaborate on this premise. Firstly, linguistic research suggests that individuals respond to issues differently depending on the linguistic frames within which issues are discussed. A second strand of research further explores the spatial influences in ethical thinking (Bachelard 1994). While Jones, for example, discusses the potential impact of proximity, this emerging strand of research explores whether an individual's sense of place may also be an important factor in ethical understanding.

These issue-related elements may help to develop an understanding of accountant's experiences of ethics and professionalism. The specific linguistic and spatial characteristics of accounting practice may be related to the way ethical issues are framed and their subsequent moral intensity experienced by professional accountants. There is a particular concern over the sanitised, technical, algorithmic language that often frames investment decisions and other ethical issues, within accounting textbooks and the accounting profession more generally. Broadbent (1998), (see also DeMoss and McCann, 1997), implies that *accounting logic* reduces moral intensity because it excludes emotion and McPhail (2001) suggests that managerial techniques dehumanise individuals by representing them as objects in technical and ethically neutral terms (See Bauman, 1996).

From this brief discussion of the descriptive/empirical ethics literature, it is possible to begin to model the complex mixture of factors that may influence how individual accountants engage with ethical dilemmas. The model shown, in figure 1.4, highlights that individual, contextual and issue related factors all play an important role in both the way accountants experience and respond to ethical issues. The following section of the report attempts to further elaborate this model by exploring the second main debate within the ethics literature. This discussion revolves around the normative question of how an individual should behave.

Normative perspectives on ethics and individual behaviour

Traditionally, moral philosophers have applied themselves to Socrates' question 'How ought I to behave?' Two prominent perspectives have developed in response to this normative analysis. One is based on the idea of duty and is termed *deontological* ethics, the other focuses on consequences and is generally referred to as the *teleological* position.

Deontological ethics

The main proponent of the deontological position is Emmanuel Kant. His argument is based on two principles: reason and respect. Kant advocated that Socrates question should be answered through deductive reasoning. When reason is applied to a dilemma, Kant suggests that actions follow a universal law. Take, for example, the issue of theft. If tempted to steal, Kant suggests that we ask ourselves whether we could accept that our children, neighbours, employees and so on also be allowed to steal at will ... from us!? Kant labels this rule the Categorical Imperative. Secondly, Kant argues that we have a duty to treat other individuals as ends in themselves and to act in a way that respects their capacity to act. Kant suggests that anyone who behaves in accordance with both these principles acts out of duty and, therefore, ethically. Rawls' 'Theory of Justice' advances the deontological position further. He suggests that while we may see the logic of the Categorical Imperative and agree that it is important to treat other human beings with respect, but that we need some help in proceduralising this principle. His solution comes in the form of a 'veil of ignorance' where deciding on a course of action that respects other individuals requires that the decision makers are placed in 'the original position' behind a veil of ignorance. From an original position of equality, not knowing what or who one might become, one is therefore compelled to respond to Socrates' proposition, by placing oneself in the position of everyone else in society, or at least each category of individual since one does not know whether one is likely to become one of these people.

While Kant's deontological response to the question of how one ought to behave is based on deductive reasoning, Rawls' position requires a different kind of moral capacity as it takes a well developed moral imagination to be able to place oneself behind the veil of ignorance or in the circumstances of each individual who might be affected by a decision.

Teleological ethics

The normative literature generally distinguishes between deontological and teleological ethical perspectives. While a deontological position focuses on the rightness or wrongness of an action in itself, a teleological position establishes the morality of a particular action by reference to the consequences of that action. Take the example discussed above. From a deontological perspective, theft may be considered morally wrong because of the kind of action it is regardless of whether or not the act produces good consequences, for example, in the case of Robin Hood. Teleologists, therefore, contend that the rightness or wrongness of an action is established by reference to its consequences. While deontological ethics is often criticised for producing rules that are too general to be helpful in specific ethical dilemmas, the teleological position is criticised because identifying every possible consequence of an action is impossible but more importantly because it can be used to justify some heinous actions. For example, a consequentialist position would allow the torture of a terrorist to save the lives of numerous others.

Virtue-based approaches to individual action

The deontological and consequentialist positions outlined above are generally termed principle-based approaches to the problem of how one should act. An alternative position is, however, provided by virtue theorists (Lovell elaborates on this branch of ethical theory in chapter four of his review). Virtue theorists contend that while it may be important to articulate certain moral principles, in practice virtue is more important than abstract philosophising (Whetstone 2001; MacIntyre, 1982; Collier 1995). Hartman (1998) comments that:

> *Virtue ethicists deny that making moral decisions is a matter of calculation as principle-based theories, particularly utilitarian ones imply ... Even if we can describe an ethical person as one whose acts conform to certain principles, it does not follow, that the best way to teach Smith to be ethical is to give her principles to follow.*

The concern of virtue theorists is that while individuals may adhere to a set of principles this does not necessarily imply that these principles are an integral part of their character (Hartman 1998; Whetstone 2001). For example, while someone may enact a certain principle, they may do so out of routine, self-interest or some other ulterior motive. It is another thing entirely to say that someone *is* courageous or loyal or honest. Hartman (1998) explains that the virtuous person is *inclined* to do the right thing. Virtue is, therefore, not about calculation, but a matter of predisposition where virtue is an element of character (Hartman, 1998; Whetstone, 2001; Shaw, 1997). It is assumed that specific virtues arise from, are given meaning by, and sustained by the broader narratives within which the individual is situated (MacIntyre 1982). Hartman (1998) comments that:

> ... a good life is an integrated life, one committed to a consistent set of values, principles, projects, people and in many cases to a community, that can give it meaning.

The argument that virtues require a broader sustaining narrative may be helpful in understanding the changing discourse surrounding accounting practice discussed later in the report. What type of virtues do these new narratives engender? Which virtues become less sustainable as they begin to lose their meaning? Francis (1990), (see also Libby and Thorne, 2004) brings virtue theory directly to bear on accounting practice when he says:

> I want to pose what I regard as the most important contemporary question facing accountants: Is accounting practice after virtue? That is, do accountants seek virtue and if so, how do they achieve it?

The literature on virtue theory provides a theoretical basis for beginning to explore some of the idealised characteristics often associated with professionals and the broader narratives that sustain these values.

Reason and moral sense theorists

The discussion of inclination in the virtue theory literature hints at a broader debate over the way that individuals should be encouraged to respond to ethical dilemmas. Some theorists suggest that reason is the only appropriate basis for ethical decision making, other theorists contend that something more is required (McNaughton, 1988). Kant represents one of the most celebrated proponents of the rational approach to ethics. He grounded ethics in reason and attempted to develop universally applicable moral principles based solely on the application of reason (Macintyre 1998; Mackie, 1977). However, Macintyre (1998) explains that while Locke similarly contended that morality could be demonstrated like a mathematical proof, Hume, on the other hand argued that reason merely furnished the individual with the facts of the matter. According to Hume, the actual act of making a moral decision required something more than reason. Macintyre (1998) also explains that the Earl of Shaftesbury and Francis Hutcheson both believed that moral distinctions depended on a moral sense rather than reason. According to Macintyre (1998), Shaftsbury represented this sense as an *inner eye* that was able to distinguish the right from the wrong. He explains Shaftsbury's position as follows:

A moral judgement is thus the expression of a response of feeling to some property of an action ... just as an aesthetic judgement is the expression of just such a response to the properties of shapes and figures.

The theorisation of the importance and role of moral sense has come a long way from Shaftsbury's inner eye. The fundamental role of empathy towards, and the core responsibility for, others has been the subject of extensive theoretical exploration both by Bauman (1996; 1993) and Levinas (Hand, 1997). A more practical analysis of what this inner eye might entail has been developed through the concept of Social and Emotional Learning (SEL) (Gardener, 1983) or emotional intelligence (McPhail, 2004). Proponents of SEL suggest that there are different categories of intelligence and that the qualities associated with emotional intelligence, for example emotional self awareness, an awareness of the emotions of others and the ability to enter into the feelings of others, can be taught (Goleman, 1995; Cohen, 1999).

The normative literature contributes towards an understanding of the ethics of individual accountants in a number of ways (see Figure 1.5). Firstly, it provides us with an insight into how accountants are explicitly and implicitly taught how they ought to behave. Conventional models of accounting practice are based on a combination of rational thinking and narrow financial consequentialism. Accountants are, therefore, exposed to this particular normative ethic during their degree programmes and professional training (Gray *et al.* 1994; McPhail, 1999). This ethic provides the normative basis for everyday accounting practice and influences the resolution of specific ethical dilemmas. While the focus of this particular report does not allow a detailed exploration of financial consequentialism, there is a considerable literature that critiques the making of ethical decisions that affect other human beings, the environment, future generations and ourselves, solely on the basis of financial consequences (see for example Carson, 1962; Daly and Cobb, 1989). The debate surrounding the role of emotion in ethical thinking and the notion of virtue provides just two aspects of this critique.

Analytical perspectives on ethics and the individual

The third main strand within the moral philosophy literature explores the fundamental basis of individual ethics. While the normative literature focuses on the question, how should I behave? the analytical literature addresses the question why is it important for individuals to behave ethically? A simple response to this question might be that individual accountants should behave ethically because the professional bodies say that they should, or because it is in the best long term interests of the profession or the individual accountant to do so. However, the analytical literature pushes the debate beyond the mere self-interest of the individual accountant, or the interest of the profession, and focuses on the broader, civic and political basis of ethical behaviour.

This section of the report briefly reviews the analytical literature to develop further insights into the issues surrounding the ethics of individual accountants. The analytical literature, for the sake of clarity, can be split into two main strands. The traditional school of thought has drawn on the work of Jean-Jacques Rousseau and his conceptualisation of the 'Social Contract,' as a political basis for individual ethical behaviour. However, a second, more critical, post-structuralist literature focuses on the operation of power through the construction of ethical subjectivity. Both strands of the literature are briefly introduced below together with the implications for understanding the ethics of individual accountants.

The individual as the basis of moral reflection

Rousseau, who is probably best known for his work on the Social Contract, changed the primary question of moral philosophy. Rousseau was not so much concerned with specific individual action, as with the more fundamental question of, 'who am I?' He suggested that the answer to this question placed the individual within a community of others (Nielsen, 1991). Rousseau contended that it was this fact, and the subsequent conclusion that our actions impinged on other individuals, that made the question, 'how should I behave,' of any relevance. At the heart of Rousseau's perspective was a concern that people viewed themselves not as isolated individuals but rather as citizens, members of a group with concomitant responsibilities towards other individuals, and civic responsibilities towards the group as a whole. As Macintyre, (1998) explains, Rousseau contended that, 'men have to learn how … they can act not as private individuals, as men, but rather as citizens'.

This particular perspective embeds the individual within a community of others, with civic responsibilities and raises some challenging questions for accountants. To what extent might accounting be construed as a civic practice? How do accountants perceive their own professional identity? and in what sense can the individual actions of accountants serve broader civic objectives?

The rights and duties of individuals

Rousseau's perspective is often used as the basis for a related discussion of individual rights and duties. These concepts represent two opposite but complementary aspects of ethical relationships between individuals and groups. Where a right relates to the way an individual can expect to be treated by others, a duty relates to the obligation towards others. There is considerable debate within the literature as to the nature of individual rights and how they are to be protected. Within financial accounting practice, property rights, in the form of share ownership, are a key motivating factor in the production of accounting reports. However, there is now a considerable body of literature that questions whether companies only have a duty to produce information for shareholders or also to other stakeholders based on other human rights (see for example Freeman, 1984; Gray, 2001 and 2002).

A key part of this debate is how individual rights are to be conceptualised and enforced. Macintyre (1998) noted that John Locke built on the work of Thomas Hobbes, and suggested that individuals should hand over their authority and power to legislative and administrative bodies, on the basis that these bodies would protect 'natural rights'. Locke argued that it was this process that gave the state its legitimacy. According to Rousseau, Hobbes and Locke, the ethics of individuals only made sense when it was set within a broader context of supporting institutions. Indeed, Hobbes suggested that for ethical rights and obligations to be sustained, the state must intervene to ensure equality in power. In other words, the principal objective of government was not to enforce individual rights, but rather to promote equality. Hobbes implied that the promotion of individual rights would emerge as a consequence of increased equality.

The accounting profession is a political institution. In its present form, it protects the rights and, therefore, serves the interests of a particular group in society. However, a growing body of literature questions whether the accounting profession might serve a broader Hobbesian function by providing a broader set of information to a greater number of stakeholders. This rebalancing of power may result in the promotion and protection of individual rights more generally.

Post-structuralist perspectives on individual ethics

In contrast to the traditional analytical literature, the post-structuralist literature draws on the work of Friedrich Nietzsche to develop a more critical analysis of the relationship between individual ethical identity and power. MacIntyre (1998) states that Nietzsche fundamentally changed the focus of conventional ethical analysis by arguing that it was morality itself that was the key problem. He was primarily concerned with the ways that individuals used moral norms to control others. Post-structuralist analysis draws on Nietzsche's basic premise to push the study of individual ethics away from questions of how an individual should behave towards the way in which notions of good and bad are developed, sustained and operate. The work of the French historian of thought, Michel Foucault, provides an example of this type of analysis (McPhail 1999). In his later work, Foucault posed the question: 'how do individuals become ethical subjects?' or, more specifically, how does 'ethical self-understanding' emerge? (see Hoy, 1994 and Hacking, 1994). This kind of ethical analysis is at a level below that of conventional moral philosophy (MacIntyre, 1998) and focuses on the underlying ethical substance that allows moral codes to function (Hoy, 1994).

Foucault's early re-conceptualisation of ethics consisted of four major elements (McPhail, 1999).

(i) **The means by which we change ourselves to become ethical subjects:** Our self-imposed discipline.

(ii) **The Telos:** the type of person we aspire to be when we behave morally.

(iii) **Ethical Substance:** that part of ourselves which is taken to be the relevant domain for ethical judgement.

(iv) **The Mode of Subjection:** the way in which individuals are incited to recognise their moral obligations. For example, some obligations may be engendered by religious invocation while others may be engendered by social convention and yet others by reasoned analysis.

Foucault uses the term self-discipline to refer to the disciplinary power that individuals exert against themselves to regulate their actions. A key aspect of Foucault's work relates to both the action and the attitude of control. Traditionally, power is conceptualised in terms of one individual or group of individuals exercising power against another less powerful individual or group. However, Foucault was interested in how individuals came to exercise power against themselves. He suggested that while an individual's experiences of control might be oppressive in the sense that they obey, but only reluctantly, the operation of power through the construction of ethical subjectivity might have less threatening connotations. An individual might in fact feel a sense of moral goodness through the kind of power that was exercised through ethical self-disciplining.

The second characteristic of Foucault's conception of ethics, the *Telos*, related to the type of aspirations individuals had when disciplining themselves to behave morally. Accountancy is conventionally taught within the rubric of marginalist economics. Within this paradigm, the corporation is responsible to society only to the extent that it maximises its own efficiency and the wealth of its shareholders. Rational economic decisions are justified purely in terms of their impact on profit.

While the kind of person that each individual accountant aspires to be probably emerges from a complex mixture of personal characteristics and circumstances, the literature suggests that notions of efficiency and wealth maximisation may be firmly embedded within the accounting *Telos* (McPhail, 1999).

The third characteristic in Foucault's conception of ethics is *ethical substance*. This element refers to those areas of our lives that we take to be the relevant domain for ethical judgement, or those parts of our lives that engage moral reasoning. Finally, the *mode of subjection* refers to the fundamental medium through which individuals recognise their moral obligations. For example, within accountancy, moral responsibilities are engendered primarily through rational, economic analysis, however, the mode of subjection could equally be religious maxims.

Foucault's work highlights the possibility that power may operate through the construction and maintenance of the ethical subjectivities of individual accountants. While this process may be viewed either in a positive or negative sense, much of the critical readings of Foucault explore the ways in which ethical subjectivities may come to serve particular interests. Indeed, the broader critical and post-structuralist literature challenge the accounting profession to reflect on exactly how power operates through professional ethics.

Summary

This section of the report has focused on the broader moral philosophy literature on the ethics of individuals. The discussion has focused around the three main strands within the literature: descriptive, normative and analytical perspectives. This section of the review has attempted to tease out, from these three broad literatures, insights that might contribute towards the understanding of the ethics of individual accountants. These insights are represented in the model in figure 1.6.

The chapter commenced by exploring empirical evidence that suggests that the ethical proclivities of individual accounting students and practising accountants are not as developed as might be expected. However, concern over ethics is not isolated to the accounting profession; there is growing unease amongst the other established professions over the ethical tendencies of their members.

The psychology literature suggests that the stilted ethical tendencies of accounting students and practitioners are specifically related to their role as accountants and that the individual experiences of professional accountants are different from their values, experiences and moral standing in other areas of their lives. Further, any discussion of the ethics of individual professional accountants must bear in mind cultural differences and also the organisational setting within which individuals are situated and that individual's experience of ethics and professionalism is likely to vary depending on their age, gender characteristics and their position within an organisation.

From this brief discussion of the descriptive/empirical ethics literature, it is possible to begin to model the complex mixture of factors that may influence how individual accountants engage with ethical dilemmas. The model shown, in figure 1.5, highlights that individual, contextual and issue-related factors all play an important role in the way accountants experience and respond to ethical issues.

Figure 1.5: Modelling professional ethics - the normative question

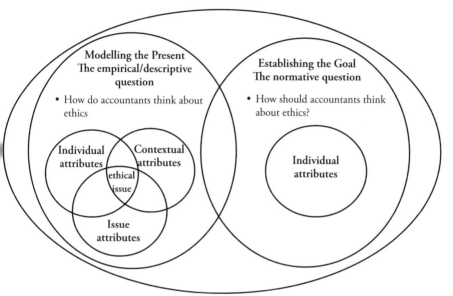

Individual attributes

- Age, Gender, Nationality
- Moral development
- Normative ethic
- Virtues
- Reason or moral sense

Contextual attributes

- Categorisation
- Organisation
- Linguistic framing
- Place
- Virtue narratives

Issue attributes

- Nature of consequences
- Social consensus
- Possibility of effect
- Temporal immediacy
- Proximity
- Concentration of effect

Individual attributes

- What level and kind of moral development?
- What normative ethic?
- What virtues?
- Reason or moral sense?

The analytical ethical literature locates the discussion of the ethics of individual accountants within its broader political economic context (see figure 1.6) whereas Rousseau's work places the ethical actions of individuals within the context of society more generally, post-structuralist analysis highlights the role of power in the construction of the ethical subjectivity of accountants and questions how concepts of good and bad might serve particular sets of interests.

Figure 1.6: Modelling professional ethics - The Analytical Question

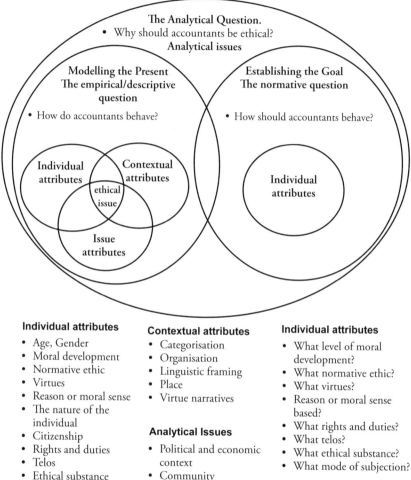

Individual attributes

- Age, Gender
- Moral development
- Normative ethic
- Virtues
- Reason or moral sense
- The nature of the individual
- Citizenship
- Rights and duties
- Telos
- Ethical substance
- Mode of subjection

Issue attributes

- Nature of consequences
- Social consensus
- Possibility of effect
- Temporal immediacy
- Proximity
- Concentration of effect

Contextual attributes

- Categorisation
- Organisation
- Linguistic framing
- Place
- Virtue narratives

Analytical Issues

- Political and economic context
- Community
- Power

Individual attributes

- What level of moral development?
- What normative ethic?
- What virtues?
- Reason or moral sense based?
- What rights and duties?
- What telos?
- What ethical substance?
- What mode of subjection?

The following chapter builds on this foundation by exploring the second main aspect of the review: professionalism as it specifically relates to individuals.

ENDNOTES:

1   Studies which have examined the influence of business education on students ethical attitudes are mixed (Arlow and Ulrich, 1980; Boyd, 1981; Martin, 1981-82; Miesing and Preble, 1985) but they are more negative than positive (Arlow 1991).

2   Tanel (1994) explains that environmental problems have had a significant impact on the increasing concern with ethics within the engineering profession.

3   Kucner (1993) talks about PET, a professional ethics training program within firms which is designed to sensitise employees to ethical issues.

4   This concern is being expressed both within and outside the profession (Smith 1990).

5   A schema is an abstract notion that refers to the knowledge structures that individuals may unconsciously employ to organise and make sense of social and organisational situations (Fiske and Kinder, 1981, in Choo 1989).

6   The metaphor of the actors/actresses script may be helpful in explaining this argument. Schemas can be thought of as a script that an actor would follow in a film. The script provides actors with an understanding of the situation and also with an idea of what they are expected to say and how they are expected to act.

CHAPTER TWO

PROFESSIONALISM AND THE INDIVIDUAL

The aim of this chapter is to explore the literature on the nature of professionalism. The following issues were identified within the literature and are discussed in more detail in this chapter.

- Theoretical views of the professions.

- Characteristics of a profession:
    - the public interest
    - independence
    - education
    - professional codes of conduct

- Historical perspectives on the accounting profession that indicate the middle class composition of the early profession might be important for understanding current developments:
    - origins
    - codification
    - competence
    - class composition
    - character

Chapter one provided a review of some of the business ethics and moral philosophy literature that contributes towards an understanding of the ethical experiences of individual accountants. This chapter focuses more specifically on the second main theme of this report, namely, professionalism. As it is quite difficult to disentangle institutional from individual dimensions of professionalism, there will, therefore, be some overlap with Aileen Pierce's complementary discussion of the ethics of professional accounting firms.

The chapter introduces various theoretical orientations to the study of the professions in general; it also provides some definitions of professionalism; a delineation of some of the main characteristics of a profession and a discussion of how these attributes relate to individual accountants. The chapter concludes by briefly exploring the origin and historical development of the accounting profession in the UK.

Theoretical views of the professions

The different theoretical approaches to exploring professions and professionalism (Roberts, 2001), inevitably influence how these concepts are perceived. Different theoretical orientations include:

(i) The sociology of the professions (*eg.* Abbott, 1988; Willmott, 1986)

(ii) Structuralist/functionalist studies (*eg.* Tinker, 1984)

(iii) Historical studies (*eg.* Walker, 1991)

(iv) Phenomenological studies (*eg.* Grey, 1998)

Studies that examine the incorporation and operation of institutionalised bodies of professionals have drawn variously and often simultaneously on functionalist, interactionist and critical theoretical perspectives. The functionalist perspective is derived primarily from the work of Durkheim (1933) and has traditionally provided the main theoretical orientation for viewing the professions (Walker, 1991; Carr-Saunders and Wilson, 1933; and Parsons, 1954, both in Edwards 2001). This perspective is based on the assumption that a profession's status and its economic rewards are directly related to the function it performs in society (Hooks, 1991). Interactionist perspectives, by contrast, view the professions as groups of individuals vying with each other for political status and economic rent (Power, 1992; Sikka and Willmott, 1995). Finally, critical perspectives study the function of the professions in relation to political and structural expediencies (See Roberts, 2001; Willmott, 1986; Johnson, 1982, in Grey, 1998). Larson (1977, in Macdonald, 1984) for example states: 'professionalism is ... an attempt to translate one order of scarce resources – specialist knowledge and skills – into another – social and economic rewards'. While a functionalist orientation might highlight the role of accountants in providing useful and credible financial information, and, in doing so, contribute towards the efficient operation of the capital markets, a critical perspective would attempt to locate this function within underlying capitalist free market ideology and as a consequence the whole gamut of its assumptions and exploitation within society.

The assumptions embedded within these different theoretical perspectives add a degree of complexity to the idea of professionalism. Most practising accountants have a vague, functionalist view of both their profession and what it means to be a professional, and as the interactionist perspective implies, may be tinted with an element of competition and even territorialism when it comes to other professions (Power, 1992). Yet many studies suggest that accountants have a very poor theoretical awareness of the specific structural function of accounting, or the political economy of accounting that is the focus of the more critical perspectives. Lovell (2005) elaborates on this in his discussion of 'the significance of the market within business ethics debates'. One might speculate that the lack of theoretical reflection on the nature of professions, particularly within the professional curriculum, could have a significant impact on individual accountants' lack of understanding of professionalism.

Characteristics of a profession

With these different theoretical perspectives in mind, this section summarises the literature on the nature of professionalism and in particular explores the defining, normative characteristics that have been associated with the professions.

Table 1 - Illustrative characteristics of a profession

Kerr *et al.* (1977)	Downie (1990)	Walker (1991)
• Autonomy;	• A knowledge base;	• An intellectual basis;
• Collegial maintenance of standards;	• Service through relationships;	• Specialist training and education; and
• Ethics;	• Social commentators (they have public interest at heart);	• A code of professional ethics; professional autonomy and altruism as opposed to self-interest.
• A feeling of responsibility to avoid self-interest and emotional involvement with clients; and	• Independence; and	
	• Education as opposed to training.	
• Professional commitment and professional identification.		

Walker (1991) suggests that a definitive set of 'professional characteristics' has proved elusive (Table 1 provides some examples of the kind of professional characteristics identified by some authors). Hall (1968, in Clikeman *et al*, 2001) defines professionalism as: 'The extent to which a person possesses attitudes such as belief in public service and a sense of calling to the field'. Mayer (1988) distinguishes between professional and bureaucratic authority. He says: 'Professional authority is based on expertise and collegiality, [it] is orientated outwards towards the community of knowledge, while bureaucratic authority is hierarchical [and] directed towards organisational survival'. Norris and Niebuhr (1983), drawing on Hall (1968) contend that professionalism has both structural and attitudinal elements. They suggest that structural aspects include: training, the formation of a professional association and the development of a code of ethics. Frankel (1989) views professions as moral communities, commenting that they: 'develop social and moral ties among their members who enter into a community of common purpose'. He states that a profession can be conceived as:

A moral community whose members are distinguished as individuals and as a group by widely shared goals and beliefs about the values of those goals ... about the appropriate means of achieving them, and about the kinds of relations which in general should prevail among themselves.

Hauptman and Hill (1991) also suggest that a profession has a body of theoretical, specialist knowledge; is committed to the public interest and has an enforceable ethical commitment and code. However, they suggest that these characteristics are often more orientated towards maintaining the legitimacy of the group rather than the interest of the common good.

The literature suggests that professionalism may also be strongly associated with regulation. Likierman (1989) points out that professions normally have some form of regulatory and disciplinary procedures to ensure that some form of public commitment is maintained. Different spheres of regulation have been identified within the literature and include:

(i) Government agencies;

(ii) Civil/professional duties;

(iii) Liability rules for malpractice; and

(iv) Complaint based systems.

From this brief review of the literature, it is possible to distinguish between the structural characteristics of a profession and the attitudinal characteristics of a professional (see Figure 2.1). However, while this distinction may be useful for engaging with the complexity of professionalism, it is somewhat artificial because structural issues influence individual perceptions and conversely individual attitudes are also reflected in professional structures.

Figure 2.1: Profession and Professional Characteristics

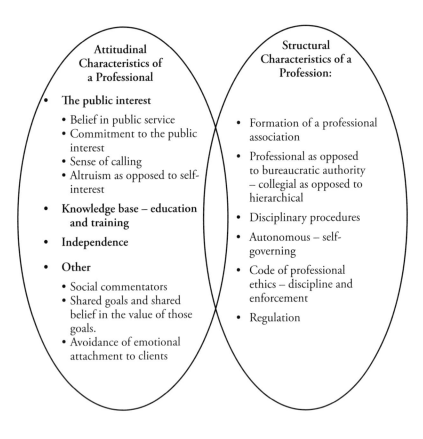

The remainder of this chapter focuses on the attitudinal characteristics of professionalism and, in particular, the public interest, independence, education and one structural characteristic, that of professional codes of conduct (for a fuller discussion of the structural characteristics of professionalism see Pierce (2006)). This is followed by a review of the historical development of the profession.

The public interest

One of the defining, ideal characteristics of a professional, is that they should have some form of commitment towards the common good (Gaa, 1990) (see Lovell's 'The significance of the individual within business ethics debates'). According to figure 2.1, four characteristics of a professional attitude are: belief in public service; commitment to the public interest; a sense of calling; and altruism as opposed to self interest. These four elements are discussed together under the term public interest.

The accounting profession claims to operate in the interests of the public. The American Institute of CPAs code of professional ethics (1988, in Claypool *et al.* 1990) for example, states that CPAs should 'act in a way that will serve the public interest, honour the public trust and demonstrate commitment to professionalism'. Sikka, Wilmott and Lowe (1989) comment that, in the UK, public interest claims are at the heart of the profession's efforts to secure its Royal Charter. For example, in its submission (1948) to attain chartered status the ICAEW stated: 'The furtherance of the aforesaid objects would be facilitated and the public interest served'. The Supplemental Royal Charter of The Institute of Chartered Accountants of Scotland also makes reference to the Institute 'being desirous of furthering ... and serving the public interest'. Lee (1995) however, contends that while the commitment to serve the public interest is one of the defining characteristics of the profession, a historical review of the professionalisation of accountancy provides evidence that accountants have used the public interest ideal as a means primarily of protecting their own economic self-interest. As such, Lee makes a distinction between the official rhetoric of professionalism and the practice of professionals.

The literature discusses what the profession means when it says that it will facilitate the public interest and whether the assumptions on which the claim is made stand up to critical scrutiny. There is little evidence that the profession has overtly and rigorously engaged with what the public interest might mean in terms of the fundamental analytical moral literature discussed above. On the contrary, Sikka, Wilmott and Lowe (1989), drawing on the profession's own conceptions, suggest that public interest was principally construed simply as the obligation to produce impartial accounting and auditing knowledge. Willmott (1989) similarly contends that the public interest function of accountants has traditionally been viewed as the role that accountants play in providing information for economic decision making and the efficient allocation of scarce resources. However, the broader analytical philosophical question of how this particular function can be morally justified does not appear to have been systematically addressed by the profession, nor is it explored within professional education.

It appears that the profession's primary claim in relation to serving the public interest is construed narrowly and simplistically in terms of ensuring that both the character and competence of those entering the profession is maintained, where character is defined by reference to middle class moral rectitude and competence is understood in narrow technical terms. There is little overt analysis, for example, of types of issues discussed within the normative literature on virtue theory, moral sense or emotional intelligence. The critical accounting literature has, however, begun to ground the profession's public interest claim in theories of democracy, rights and analytical moral philosophy. Dillard and Yuthus (2002) define professionalism and its relationship to the public interest by using stakeholder theory and a responsibility ethic. Westra (1986) similarly draws on the analytical philosophy literature to explore the question of: 'to whom does the accountant owe a duty?' He suggests that the answer to this question depends upon the designation of the agent. Loeb (1991) also contends that the identity of the client is of overriding importance. He comments that:

> ... *the question of what constitutes ethical behaviour ... will depend on the relation within which such behaviour is to be deployed.* (Westra, 1986).

For example, how should the client be construed. Should the client be taken to mean the corporation, a particular public sector or society in general?

Of particular concern within the accounting literature is the apparent inability of accounting students to critically engage with the concept of the public interest. While the curricula of most of the accounting professional bodies focuses on technical competence, the intellectual skills that would enable students to critically engage with the "public good" appear to be lacking in many cases (Gray *et al.* 1994).

To summarise, although the accounting profession claims to be operating in the public interest, the literature suggests that this ideal may be interpreted in a very narrow and simplistic way by professional accountants. There is little evidence of any serious analytical, ethical reflection on how accounting contributes towards a more democratic or just society and, therefore, the public interest, as opposed to the interests of a small section of society.

Independence

To the extent that there is any articulation of the public interest within the profession, it is equated with independence. For example, independence is the first rule in the AICPA's (1989) Code of Professional

Conduct (Claypool *et al.* 1990). Claypool *et al.* (1990) contend that it is 'the key ethical concept'. Everett *et al.* (forthcoming) comment on how the Canadian CA's conception of independence historically evolved to dominate their discourse on ethics. Yet within this discourse, professional independence is restricted to just single-client dependency, non-audit services and the separation of business and professional relationships (Likierman 1989). Bruce (1996) also hints that, even these narrow conceptions of independence have often lacked substance. He comments: 'stating that you are independent is no longer enough'. (See Hauptman and Hill, 1991; AICPA, 1988; Waples and Shaub, 1991; Gaa, 1990; Stanga and Turpen, 1991; McCabe *et al*, 1991; Modic, 1987, in Davis and Welton, 1991). Sikka and Willmott (1995) explore the tactics that the UK profession has employed in order to defend its 'aura' of independence and suggest that these tactics have included modifying its ethical guidelines and its disciplinary proceedings. They suggest that these changes are primarily motivated by a concern to ward off any threat to self-regulation. Zeff (1989) concedes that significant structural changes have been proposed in the US, particularly in relation to the composition of the board of trustees of the Financial Accounting Foundation. However, he also draws on Arthur Andersen *et al*'s (1991) 'The Public Accounting Profession: Meeting the Needs of a Changing World' to argue that the profession in the US has tactically attempted to narrow the scope of independence.

The recent provisions of the Sarbanes-Oxley Act, implemented partly in response to the Enron debacle (Cullinan, 2004), construes audit independence as a structural issue. While new legislative provisions may mean that individual accountant's experiences of independence, through the structures and organisation of office practice are likely to change, it is unlikely that these changes will help individual accountants ethically manage often subtle and complex conflicts of interest in specific circumstances. Nor will it contribute towards their capacity to critically engage with independence as a moral concept at the political economic level. To what extent can the normal everyday practice of accounting be considered to be independent, and should it be? According to some of the analytical literature discussed above, to remain independent and not to side with the marginalised, the impoverished or oppressed, may be both immoral and against the general public interest.

The idea of independence becomes even more problematic when viewed within the broader socio-political arena of the analytical moral philosophy literature. If accounting practice is based primarily on the property rights of capital owners, to the exclusion of the rights of others, then in what sense can professional accountants be said to be independent? From a post-structuralist perspective, the operation of power is so pervasive that any talk of independence reflects a misunderstanding of the nature of ethical subjectivity. The notion of independence, like the public interest, again seems to be interpreted within a very narrow set of boundaries.

Education

Mayer (1988; Abbott, 1983, 1988; Macdonald, 1984) suggests that education in a specific body of knowledge is a key aspect of professional identity. Walker (1991) similarly explains that the establishment of certain educational criteria for entrance to a profession helps to establish its credibility[1].

However, there is some concern that accounting education is overly technical in its orientation. Gray *et al.* (1994; see also Fleming, 1996) contend that the accounting profession places too much emphasis on the technical abilities of students at the expense (and perhaps even to the detriment) of their ethical and intellectual development. Fleming (1996), for example, shows that of a total of 400 marks in the final stage of the ICAEW examinations that he analysed, only 6.66 marks, less than 2% of the total available, related to ethical issues. Not surprisingly, the ethical issues considered were mainly to do with independence and confidentiality.

The AICPA responded to these concerns by extending the period of study required prior to sitting the CPA exams[2]. The AICPA's commission on Professional Accounting Education (1983, in Clikeman *et al.* 2001) inferred that the aim behind the increase in education was to indirectly enhance students' professional awareness and professional commitment and meant that students studied for five years as opposed to four years. However, as Clikeman *et al.* (2001) points out, simply increasing the quantity of education is unlikely to have any impact on students' 'professional commitment, ethical orientation and professionalism'. The fact that the commission stated that the reasoning behind the increase was to bring accounting more in line with professions like law may imply that the changes served a symbolic rather than a substantive function.

The discussion of accounting education implies that individual accountants' experiences of professionalism are oriented towards a sense of technical competence. Of course technical ability is important, and the literature suggests that one of the defining normative characteristics of a profession is the ability to take technical know-how and identify how it can be applied in new ways for the benefit of society in general. There is, however, little evidence that the professional curriculum fosters this kind of broader political-economic understanding that is necessary for this type of professional thinking to emerge. There is also little evidence that the profession has engaged with the broader questions raised by the normative moral philosophy literature. While the professions code of conduct delineates a list of rules, there is little theoretical analysis of how accountants should behave and even less discussion of the mode of education required to support these values.

Professional codes of conduct

Abbott (1983) argues that: 'Ethics codes are the most concrete cultural form in which professions acknowledge their societal obligations'. He says: 'You can't be a profession without having professional ethics'

(Abbott, 1983, in Neu and T'Aerien, 2000). Claypool *et al.* (1990) argue that self-regulation by a code of ethics is a primary characteristic of a profession. These codes are generally associated with a complaint-based enforcement system where members report any instances where they become aware of misdemeanours (Beets and Killough, 1990). However, the literature suggests that professionals are generally reluctant to report breaches by their fellow practitioners (Bayles, 1987, in Beets and Killough, 1990).

Preston *et al.* (1995) (see also Jamal and Bowie, 1995; Backof and Martin, 1991) argue that the accounting profession's code of ethics serves a legitimating function and Huff and Kelly (1989) suggest that the American Accounting Association's 1988 revised code of practice and its associated 'practice-monitoring programme' represented a specific attempt to address growing public concerns over substandard audit work. Parker (1994) concludes that these codes have a dual function and serve both public and private interests. He says that:

> *While encouraging a sense of social responsibility in the professional member, they also provide justification for professional self-interest … while their standards and pronouncements are couched in terms of the public interest, they appear to be inextricably bound up in the profession's private interest.* (Parker, 1994; Willmott, 1986).

However, while codes of professional conduct have been identified as a structural characteristic in Figure 2.1 a significant part of the literature discusses the impact of these codes on individual professionals' attitudes towards ethics. The literature distinguishes between different types of codes that may influence the perceptions of individual accountants. Frankel (1989) identifies three forms of professional codes: aspirational, educational and regulatory. Claypool *et al.* (1990) also distinguish between 'broad principles' and 'enforceable rules'. Most of the professional accounting institutes' ethical guidelines find expression in both principles and rules. Broader aspirational principles can be found in CIMA's bye-laws, for example, which warn members against 'dishonourable or unprofessional conduct' and its Ethical Guidelines require accountants to: 'refrain from any conduct which might bring discredit to the profession'. Similarly, the ACCA requires accountants to: 'refrain from ... misconduct which ... [is] likely to bring discredit to themselves, the Association or the accountancy profession' (Fleming, 1996). Ruland and Lindblom (1992) seem to convey a related distinction when they discuss the difference between implicit and explicit expectations. They define explicit rules as those outlined in professional codes of conduct. Implicit rules, by contrast, are derived societal expectations in relation to professionals' roles in society. Ruland and Lindblom (1992) contend that the AICPA's code contains examples of both explicit rules and implicit principles[3].

While the enforceable rules-based elements of these codes are reflections of the broader aspirational principles, it is obvious that these principles represent an expectation of something more, something beyond mere rule following. Yet despite the observation that professional accounting codes contain aspirational elements, Likierman (1989) contends that there are a number of 'accepted professional dilemmas' and that these are generally 'routine' and 'deal with the way in which the profession seeks to maintain its good name'. For example, the CPA's reactions to ethical dilemmas are primarily governed by deference to its professional code of ethics, rather than an ideal notion of professionalism (Claypool *et al.* 1990). Brooks (1989) also contends that the main source of guidance for accountants is found in the code of conduct.

Velayuthan (2003) suggests that the accounting profession's code of ethics has, over time, moved from a focus on moral responsibility for a public good to that of technical specification for a product or service. This reflects a change in public values where technique has replaced character as an important virtue[4] (Velayutham, 2003). Mitchell and Sikka (1993), however, suggest a more pragmatic possibility and contend that focusing on the technical aspects of accounting also serves to protect it from governmental interference. This is not to imply that a particular set of aspirational notions, prevalent a few decades ago, in themselves are any better or worse than a codified set of principles. The issue is the *way* in which ethical dilemmas and professionalism are experienced, not the specific values themselves. Harris and Brown (1990) explain that relying on codified rules and the deference to some external authority represents a relatively low level of ethical awareness. The cognitive moral development literature discussed above supports this claim. ICAS's (2004) study suggests that many ICAS members adopt a rule-based, as opposed to a principles-based, approach to ethical decision making. However, there is a significant discussion of the detrimental impact of rule-based approaches on ethical development within the literature. Dillard and Yuthus (2002) state that: 'resolutions of ethical dilemmas has become an exercise in rule following'. It is generally considered that such rule-based approaches impede ethical development because they remove the requirement to choose between competing alternative courses of actions and to accept responsibility for those actions. The combination of technical education and ethical rule following is of particular concern to many commentators as they suggest that these characteristics combine to work against the kind of independent analytical thinking that is crucial for moral development as they conceive it. The codified rule-based aspect of ethical codes may therefore, paradoxically, work against aspirational principles.

Fisher (1999) labels the rules-based approach a 'rational choice' view of ethics and Fogarty (1997) claims that this approach emanates from the pervasiveness of rational, scientific ways of thinking. The normative ethics literature highlights the debate over how individuals should be encouraged to respond to ethical dilemmas. While on the one hand the rational school of thought promotes reason as the only appropriate basis of ethical decision making, the moral sense school of thought suggests that some form of emotional response must take precedence (McNaughton, 1988). Fogarty thus infers that the profession's approach to ethics is very firmly grounded in a rational view of ethical decision making. Yet, as Jensen and Wygant (1990) suggest, professionals need to deal with circumstances when the rules either do not, or should not, apply and conclude that accountants need to act out of a *sense* of what is right or wrong.

However, the empirical evidence suggests that ethical codes often have little practical impact on professionals in practice. ICAS (2004) for example comments that ICAS's code of professional conduct 'did not appear to actively or self consciously form part of the daily decision making of accountants'. Some studies suggest that members may not even be aware of the codes to which they are obliged to adhere (see for example Baldick, 1980; Davis, 1984; Hughson and Kohn, 1980, in Beets and Killough, 1990) and that accountants often draw more on factors in their business environment to help with ethical decision making rather than resources offered by their profession[5] (Cooper and Frank, 1997).

Historical perspectives on the accounting profession

The previous section presented some of the defining, normative attributes which characterise a professional attitude. This section specifically focuses on the personal characteristics associated with professional accountants and the early composition of the profession in an attempt to shed a little more light on individual professional attitudes. The structural history of the origin and development of the profession is developed more fully in Pierce (2006).

The origins of the profession

There is a considerable amount of literature on the formation and development of professional bodies and the spread of such organisations in general (see Preston *et al.* 1995; Moore and Gaffikin, 1994). The reasons behind the professionalisation of accounting are complex and any analysis of this process will be driven by the methodological perspective adopted. Thus, while some theoretical positions attribute altruistic motives to vocational groups (Carr-Saunders and Wilson, 1933; West, 1996) others present a more critical perspective on the emergence of the professions and the motivations of professionals. Larson, for example, argues that professionalism is driven by a desire to gain control of an occupational service to the exclusion of others by presenting others as being incapable of the task (Lee, 1995). Wilmott (1986) similarly argues that professionalisation is driven primarily by economic motives (see also West, 1996). He contends that: 'professional formation is a socio-political process which may be motivated by the desire for economic rewards'.

The remainder of this chapter summarises some of the critical histories of the origin of the profession in an attempt to develop some understanding of how conceptualisations of the public interest, ideas about education and codes of conduct may have initially emerged. The discussion is presented under four headings: *competence; character; codification;* and *class.*

Competence

The professionalisation of accountants in Scotland began around the mid 1800s (Kedslie, 1990; Walker, 1995, 2005b; see also Walker 2004a). In 1853 the Edinburgh accountants petitioned Queen Victoria to form The Society of Accountants in Edinburgh. Their submission was couched in terms of the public interest as opposed to the groups' own economic benefits (Lee, 1995). The public interest was principally construed in terms of ensuring that accountants were properly qualified for the job (Lee, 1995) and that the competence of accountants would be assured through entry qualifications (Kedslie, 1990; Lee, 1995).

In the US, accountants attempted to legitimise accounting education by developing university degrees early in the 1900s (Langenderfer, 1987;

Carey, 1970; Previts and Merino, 1979 in Lee, 1995). This route contrasted with the approach in the UK which was based on part-time non-university study and apprenticeship.

Historically, the public interest was identified with technical competence. From the beginning, the system of professional education reinforced a view of the professional as someone who was technically competent in the practices of accounting, rather than a civic actor with a broader socio-political understanding of the function of accounting, capable of adapting their skills to the democratic ideals of society.

Character

While the early accountants argued that the formation of a Chartered Society would benefit the public interest, some researchers have suggested that the process was initiated in part by a concern over changes in bankruptcy laws that would have threatened a lucrative business for practising accountants[6]. The effect of these changes would have placed the administration of bankruptcies in the hands of the Sheriff Clerk, a legal officer. At that time accountants dealt with over 80% of bankruptcy cases in Scotland. The accountants were successful in challenging this aspect of the law (Kedslie, 1990) and as a result of extensive lobbying, The Bankruptcy Act of 1831 allowed accountants to be appointed as official assignees in bankruptcy cases. One of the most prominent assignees appointed by the Lord Chancellor was a man called Peter Abbott. Unfortunately Abbott turned out to be a crook, and perpetrated one of the profession's earliest recorded frauds (see also Walker 1996). The appointment of assignees was based on a rather nebulous and unspecified notion of *character* (Edwards, 2001) which was loosely associated with an individual's ability to pay professional dues. The ability to pay the entrance fee to the profession was, therefore, a loose proxy for social standing which in turn was assumed to guarantee an appropriate character (Kedslie, 1990; Lee, 1995).

Codification

The profession reacted to the Abbott crisis by establishing a new supervisory, or watchdog, position (Edwards, 2001). It also started to formalise professional behaviour in professional codes of conduct (Walker 1996). While initially, professionalism was seen as something that was internal to the individual, and not something that was written down or explicit, when faced with a crisis, the profession soon attempted to codify what it meant to be a professional accountant.

Class composition

Both the Glasgow and Edinburgh societies set up entrance exams, but professionalism was bound up in class-consciousness (West, 1996; see also Macdonald, 1984) and applicants were more likely to be accepted if they were 'men of acceptable middle class characteristics' (Macdonald, 1984; see also Walker, 1988 in Lee, 1995). Macdonald (1984), for example, comments:

> … the accountancy profession in Scotland was able to place the cachet of ascription on its members because its leaders were associated with the gentry, the legal profession and the more respectable part of the bourgeoisie.

Kedslie (1990) similarly argues that the early members of the Edinburgh society were predominately upper to middle class. Entrance to the profession depended upon the member's 'suitability' for admission and the ability to pay for indentureship was an important sign of social standing and character. Lee (1995) concludes that: 'organised professions were a means by which the middle class exercised cultural control and established its social status' (see also Bledstein, 1976 and Downie, 1990).

As well as its white middle-class orientation the historical development of the idea of professionalism also reflected gender divisions (Hammond, 2002). Kirkham and Loft (1993; see also Shackleton, 1999) contend that:

> ... *the process of demarcation of accounting tasks not only reflected gender relations ... but helped give meaning to professional accountants.*

Grey's (1998) phenomenological study of being 'a professional in a big six firm' takes the understanding of character and its association with class a step further. He concluded that the meaning of being a professional was primarily bound up with a series of ways of self-conduct rather than with issues of technical competence. He argues that: 'the meaning of being a professional emerges as being embedded in a series of issues such as fairness, appearance, gender, sexuality and hierarchy'. As such, Grey suggested that professionalism was related in a phenomenological way to the language, appearance and structures of middle-class consciousness (see Fogarty, 1992, in Grey, 1998).

Neu and T'Aerien (2000) sum up the lessons from the historical development of the profession and state that: 'Accountants, like the rest of us, appear to have just made it up as they went along'. While this conclusion is perhaps a little purposive in its tone, it seems that professional attributes were more assumed in the early stages of the professionalisation of accountants and that it is only more recently that terms like professionalism, professional ethics and the public interest have been opened up to critical academic scrutiny. Neu and T'Aerien (2000) contend that:

> *It looks like ... the profession saw professional ethics as a simple extension of personal, individual morals – transposing codes of individual moral conduct ("moral rectitude", "honesty") to the collectivity without examining the behaviour of the body of accountants as a whole in the context of the larger society and the*

effects of its function on the well-being of society in general. ...
Individual moral behaviour became professional ethics.

Mitchell and Sikka (1993) similarly comment that: 'much of
the power of the accountancy profession is sustained by myths of
professionalism' (Millerson, 1964; Richards, 1984, in Mitchell and
Sikka, 1993).

An awareness of the historical development of the accounting
profession contributes towards an understanding of individual
accountant's experience of professionalism (see figure 2.2) and indicates
that professionalism was loosely related to character and that this in turn
was influenced by middle class views of respectability. Early conceptions
of the public interest, around the time of the origin of the profession,
were articulated in terms of ensuring that those entering the profession
were of an appropriate character. As Neu and T'Aerien (2000) suggest,
this focus on individual morality, rather than the collective function of
a body of professional accountants within broader society, represents
a very narrow view of the public interest and what it means to be a
professional accountant.

Figure 2.2:Modelling professional ethics - Professionalism

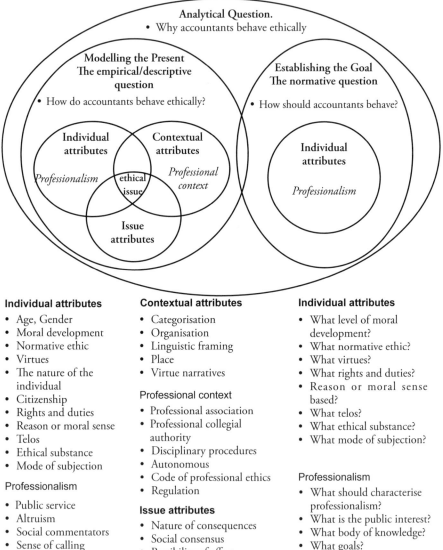

Individual attributes
- Age, Gender
- Moral development
- Normative ethic
- Virtues
- The nature of the individual
- Citizenship
- Rights and duties
- Reason or moral sense
- Telos
- Ethical substance
- Mode of subjection

Professionalism
- Public service
- Altruism
- Social commentators
- Sense of calling
- Shared goals
- Knowledge
- Independence

Contextual attributes
- Categorisation
- Organisation
- Linguistic framing
- Place
- Virtue narratives

Professional context
- Professional association
- Professional collegial authority
- Disciplinary procedures
- Autonomous
- Code of professional ethics
- Regulation

Issue attributes
- Nature of consequences
- Social consensus
- Possibility of effect
- Temporal immediacy
- Proximity
- Concentration of effect

Individual attributes
- What level of moral development?
- What normative ethic?
- What virtues?
- What rights and duties?
- Reason or moral sense based?
- What telos?
- What ethical substance?
- What mode of subjection?

Professionalism
- What should characterise professionalism?
- What is the public interest?
- What body of knowledge?
- What goals?

Summary

This brief review of the historical development of the profession provides some insights into some of the critical debates over the nature of public interest and accounting education and demonstrates that current concerns over the nature of professional attributes may have their roots in the origin of the profession. This literature certainly does not give the impression that accounting was once based on nobler democratic or civic ideals which have subsequently been lost.

This chapter has delineated some of the defining, normative characteristics traditionally associated with the idea of professionalism such as: a commitment to the public interest; a coherent body of knowledge; independence and a code of conduct. However, while the accountancy profession appears to possess these characteristics, they seem to lack substance, especially when viewed in light of the analytical moral philosophy literature. Some authors have expressed concern that professional education might produce accountants with only a narrow technical orientation and that professional codes of ethics may stultify accountants' moral development. There is also significant concern over the simplistic way in which accountants construe their professional commitment to serve the public interest and the apparent inability of accountants to engage with the broader political economy within which accounting functions (See Lovell's discussion of the market in business ethics debates).

ENDNOTES:

---

[1] There is some discussion within the literature of the difficulties that the accounting profession has experienced in establishing a coherent body of knowledge (Dyckman, 1974, in Lee, 1995).

[2] This followed the introduction of CPE in the US in the late 1960's (See Hubbard *et al.* 1989, in Fogarty, 1997).

[3] Lovell (2005) also discusses the contemporary development in inter-institutional codes of ethics.

[4] This work is based on the ICANZ and ASCPA codes.

[5] Business environment refers to the impact of the informal organisational climate, for example immediate boss, company culture and so on.

[6] Preston *et al.* (1995) present a different story of the origin and development of the profession in the US that draws on a critical, functionalist view of the professions. They suggest that the excesses of *laissez-faire* economic policy lead to calls for an independent accounting profession in the US (Preston *et al.* 1995; Moore and Gaffikin, 1994). As such, they imply that the formation of the US professional accounting bodies was driven more by demand and economic expediency than the self interest of individual accountants *per se.*

CHAPTER THREE

EVENTS IMPACTING ON PROFESSIONALISM

This section explores some historical shifts that may have had an impact on individual experiences of ethics. The issues are discussed under the following themes:

- Moral confusion;

- General reduction in trust;

- Changing societal expectations of business;

- The increased importance and complexity of accountancy;

- The commercialisation of accountancy; and

- Developments in accounting education.

While debates over whether accountants can legitimately claim to be professionals can be traced back to the origin of the profession, subsequent historical changes may also have impacted upon individual accountants' perceptions of their professional identities. This chapter outlines some of the changes that specifically relate to individual concepts of professionalism. For a further exploration of structural changes and transformations at the firm level see Pierce (2006)[1].

Moral confusion

Perhaps one of the most significant changes that has impacted on concepts of professionalism has been what MacIntyre calls the spread of 'moral confusion,' (see Davis and Welton, 1991). Williams (1995) draws on MacIntyre's *After Virtue* (1982) to suggest that the American Anthropological Association's (AAA) ethics project, which it commenced in 1988, can be understood as emerging from and a response to a broader culture of 'moral confusion' (see also Williams, *et al.* 1988; Schultz, 1989; Sundem, 1989). Williams states that:

> *The modernisation of society has destroyed the traditional societies in which moral obligations were relatively easy to understand and fulfil since the moral rules were prescribed by religious and cultural traditions and were applied by and to persons who were largely known to each other.*

Touche Ross's (1988, in Davis and Welton, 1991; see also Forisha and Forisha, 1976) study of the deteriorating standards within the profession likewise contends that society in general is partially responsible for a general decline in professional ethics. This malaise is ascribed to a 'decay in social and cultural institutions'.

Ethical development and character formation does take place in the home and primary school (Rohatyn, 1987). However, it would be misguided to suggest that primary schools and the church rather than business schools and universities, are solely responsible for increasing moral confusion. It would be equally wrong, both in moral and pragmatic terms to suggest that these institutions alone, rather than university departments and business schools, should take sole responsibility for reversing the decline. While this argument is ultimately misconstrued, not least because empirical studies indicate that accounting and business education can have a major impact on student's moral tendencies both for good and for bad, the underlying premise, that shifting notions of professionalism reflect fundamental socio-cultural changes is correct. Systems of values and beliefs are sustained by socio-cultural narratives which were traditionally embedded within social structures and institutions (MacIntyre, 1982). When these narratives were disrupted, the values that they supported began to loose their grounding and this may shed light on the early history of the professionalisation of accounting and, in particular, the implied relationship between character and class, no matter how misconstrued this may have been.

General reduction in trust

Other sections of the literature also point to a major socio-cultural shift in the way that individuals related to each other and to the professions and professionals (Unerman and O'Dwyer, 2004). In a study by Modic (1987) 51% of respondents said they trusted people less today than they did a few years ago. Bruce (1996) concludes 'the age of deference is over'; people are not willing to simply accept what those in authority say. This shift away from a reverence for, and a deference towards, the professions is reconstructing professionals as equal partners. Professionalism was traditionally construed in terms of character and social standing, but in the postmodern society there is a slippage away from the anchoring points in traditional society and this decoupling may have had significant consequences for professional accountants.

Changing societal expectations of business

Traditionally, societal expectations of business was, in the words of Milton Friedman, to make profit (in Jensen & Wygant, 1990; see also, Arlow, 1991; Magnet, 1986). However, there has been a perceptible shift in public attitude with a major body of literature attesting to a significant move towards corporate social responsibility (CSR) (Gray, 2002, 2001; Lovell also elaborates on thee changes in chapter four of his review). While there is considerable debate as to whether this discourse is likely to produce any substantive change in business practice, the emergence of social and environmental accounting as a valid academic subject and the growing momentum of CSR provides significant challenges for the scope of professional responsibility (Gray, 2001). CSR related issues have a very real impact on accounting practice at present, for example in the case of contingent liabilities. However, at a more fundamental level CSR also challenges the underlying notion about the function that accounting should serve in society, particularly in relation to its claim to be serving the public interest.

The increased importance and complexity of accountancy

Another significant shift that can be inferred from the literature is the increasingly important role that accountancy is playing in the economic well-being of both Western developed economics and also emerging economies (Lee, 1995). There has been a general increase in the scope of the financial markets and dependence on them and this in turn places extra importance on the accounting function (Brooks, 1989; see also Unerman and O'Dwyer, 2004). However, the increased importance of accounting is coupled with the increased complexity in business practice (Brooks, 1989). Intangibles, complex financial instruments and pensions are just a few problems that the accounting profession is struggling to resolve. While this increased technical complexity has focused attention on the competence of accountants and the profession's requisite body of knowledge, these issues also create problems for the profession's public interest claims. For example, while resolving how companies account for pensions requires a fairly advanced level of technical competence, the emotive and very civic nature of the issue also creates problems for the profession's claim to be acting in the public interest. This issue is summed up by Mitchell and Sikka (1993) who comment that: 'accountancy has become more pervasive at the same time as we are wondering what it means'.

The increased pervasiveness of accounting, and that of accountability, has also encroached upon professional practice. The demise in trust and respect for authority has led to calls for the accounting profession itself to be more publicly accountable (Mitchell and Sikka, 1993). However, the pervasiveness of accounting has also had an impact within accounting practices where Grey (1998), for example, talks about the use of staff evaluation forms and customer billing schedules in large accounting practices. These practices in general, along with the specific criteria against which accountants are appraised, has undoubtedly had an impact upon the idea of professionalism and on the commercialisation of the profession more generally.

The commercialisation of accountancy

There is a significant amount of discussion on the increasingly commercial orientation of accounting professionalism (Carmichael and Swieringa, 1968). Roberts (2001) comments on the contrast between the traditional role of a professional and: 'the profession's decision to compete in a commercial marketplace in a wide variety of professional services'. He states that: 'In an effort to earn extra revenues, auditors now offer almost any scheme and service' (Hanlon, 1994) and increasingly use marketing techniques. Further, Mitchell and Sikka (1993) claim that audits are now used as loss leaders to attract other more lucrative business. Roberts (2001) states that the US practitioner literature is replete with evidence that commercialism is of primary importance to CPA firms (see Craig, 1994; Nassuti, 1994) and that this commercial re-orientation is primarily driven by declining profit margins (Fraser, 1997). There is some concern that the pursuit of commercial objectives has had a detrimental impact on the quality of audit services. In his 1987 study for example, Larson referred to a number of surveys that indicated that 30-40% of all audits undertaken in the US were substandard[2] (see also M B Armstrong, 1987; Hooks, 1991).

According to Hanlon (1994, 1996) the increasing commercialisation of accounting practice reflected a broader societal shift in the expectations surrounding professional work and the way that it was appraised. Craig (1994) discussed the need to provide non-audit services for partnerships to 'succeed' and concluded that: 'the importance of these new services has changed the mindset of practitioners'. Boland (1982) questioned this commercialisation of the accounting profession, highlighting the way that growth was used as an indicator of both practice and individual success. Increased commercialisation, combined with greater litigation has resulted in most of the major accounting practices converting to limited liability firms (Lee, 1995). Roberts (2001) also suggests that this focus on commercial services has contributed towards the consolidation of accounting firms and the merger of accounting and law firms and argues that this process has had a profound impact on the mentality of American CPAs. Fraser (1997) for example quotes Ron Silberstein, an American CPA who notes that: 'When someone sitting next to me on a plane asks me what I do, I usually tell him or her I'm a salesman. Then they ask, "What do you sell?" and I tell them, "Accounting Services"'. Fraser (1997) also recounts a similar comment by Stanley Nasberg, another American CPA, who stated that: 'We have arrived because we no longer think of ourselves as merely a profession, we are a business, we are entrepreneurs'. Both these quotes extol commercial acumen and seem very far removed from the ideals of public service and altruism traditionally associated with professionalism. The implication is that the value of being seen to be a professional has somehow diminished. For these accountants at least, commercial acumen appears to be more useful than *mere* professional status. Indeed Roberts (2001) suggests that accounting, more generally, has become de-professionalised (see Zeff, 1987; Briloff, 1990 in Roberts, 2001).

However, it would be wrong to suggest that these views are ubiquitous across the profession. Rather, there are hints that this new commercialism does not sit well with more established traditional views. This tension can be seen in the following quote from Bruce (1996), who notes that: 'there were worries that some of the new generation of partners were young marketeers more concerned with profit, less loyal to colleges than senior partners and more likely to use others instrumentally for their own ambitions'. Bruce (1996) also suggests that a purely commercial view of the accounting profession is too simplistic. He comments on a study by Goodwin that argued that: 'The accountancy firm … presents an interesting hybrid of contemporary commercialism and a more traditional professionalism with an emphasis on high standards'. Bruce contends that accountants 'have to wrestle with two sides to their central identity. They are business [people], but they are also aloof, dispassionate, independent professionals'.

This conflict creates a serious problem for the profession because these identities are orientated towards two quite fundamentally different sets of interests; those of business executives rather than professionals (Dyckman, 1974, in Lee, 1995). Radcliffe *et al.* (see also Willmott and Sikka, 1997) argue that commercialism and professionalism are incompatible[3]. They specifically argue that the process of commercialisation contradicts the idea of professionalism because it represents the pursuit of self-interest over the public interest. While it is obviously possible to theoretically reconcile public and private interest within a free market, utilitarian ethical model, this prevailing worldview cannot accommodate the potential conflict of interest that the provision of both audit and consultancy services creates in practice (Schulte, 1966). Roberts (2001) concludes that increasing commercialism detracts from the accountant's fiduciary responsibilities and ultimately brings their claim to professionalism into question (although, see Downie, 1990).

Thus, there appears to be considerable concern over the increasing commercial orientation of the accountancy profession and the impact that this is likely to have on an individual accountant's professional identity. This issue is also reflected in ICAS's (2004) survey of ICAS members. They found that financial pressure, particularly from peers, was a significant concern amongst practising accountants. However, it is important to point out that this re-orientation is not peculiar to accountancy. Bruneau (1994; see also Grigg, 1993) for example, argues the engineering profession has also been handed over to the forces of the free market.

Developments in accounting education

Education is a key characteristic of a profession and over the past few decades the concept of professionalism and ethics has begun to be explored in more detail within the academic literature and business schools. During the period 1960-1973, a 'discourse promoting individualism, competitive behaviour, material acquisitiveness, and a scarcity of literature advocating business ethics, moral concerns, or responsibility for community rather than self' was evident (Lehman, 1988). Lehman contends that accounting education has traditionally been technical in nature; 'accounting students are trained in how to do'. However, her observations were accompanied by an appeal to academics to develop new forms of accounting education that would promote ethical discussion, awareness and analysis.

Williams (2004) suggests that accounting education has responded to this challenge and has begun to change. He talks about the increased focus on ethics in academic and professional terms, particularly in response to the AAA 1988 ethics project and concludes that 'accounting as an academic discipline ... has undergone a rather dramatic change in recent years'. He suggests that it has been released from economic hegemony and opened up to debate, discussion and investigation (see Williams, et al. 1988; Schultz, 1989; Sundem, 1989). Lee (1995) points out that this shift may be partially attributable to the changing nature of the academic accountancy community. He suggests that it has changed from practice-based teaching by part-time practitioners to a profession of full time teachers and researchers. Van Luijk (1990) similarly discusses the development of business ethics in particular as a subject evidenced by the number of chairs in business ethics, centres for business ethics and business ethics networks that have emerged over the past few years. Lovell's (2005) review of ethics in business provides a comprehensive overview of the theoretical developments in this area.

Although the subject remains relatively under-developed in comparison to other disciplines, for example bioethics, these developments imply that the socio-political function of accounting is now being exposed to more detailed intellectual scrutiny within business schools and that the rather nebulous concept of the public interest (Neu and T'Aerien, 2000; Esland, 1980, in Mayer, 1988) is being opened up to debate and critical analysis. Academics are now struggling with what professionalism means and the results of these explorations are, in many cases, being passed on to students through new ethics-based critical, social and environmental courses (McDonald, 1992, McPhail, 2002; 2003). Thus, the increasing commercial orientation of accounting practice can be contrasted with the increased philosophical exploration of both the political economy of accounting and the concept of the public interest (See Lovell's discussion of the market and the individual).

Summary

This chapter has briefly discussed six broad historical shifts which may have influenced individual accountants' perceptions of what it means to be a professional. Increasing moral confusion may have had an impact on the normative way in which accountants respond to ethical dilemmas. Some of the literature also expresses concern over the emergence of commercialism as perhaps the most dominant new socio-cultural factor and, as such, the basis for a potentially anti-social (or anti-civil society) reconfiguration of professionalism. According to the literature, this shift away from old civic notions of professionalism seems to jar both with the increased pervasiveness of accounting into all areas of society and the general increase in societal expectations for businesses to be more socially responsible.

The incongruity of both these trends has been most clearly seen in the Enron debacle, which brought down Andersens and threw the profession into crisis. Whether Enron will have a substantive and long-term impact on accountants' ideas about what it means to be a professional remains to be seen. Certainly, one would expect that in a social constructionist sense, both the immediate discourse surrounding the Enron debacle and the concomitant changes in both the discourse and practice of audit as a result of the Enron case are likely to have an impact. Yet, given the circumstances surrounding the collapse, if the accounting academy continues to develop, teach and promote its political-economic understanding of accounting and the public interest, then there is, in Enron at least, the potential of a more substantive change in what it means to be a professional accountant (Williams, 2004).

Endnotes:

[1] Pierce (2006) also provides an extensive discussion of the Enron case, although, the discourse surrounding this fiasco may also have an impact on individual notions of professionalism.

[2] Perhaps in response to these problems the American Accounting Association developed a new code of professional ethics in 1988. The code was accompanied by a 'practice-monitoring programme'. This quality review exercise represented an attempt to address growing public concerns over substandard audit work (Huff and Kelly, 1989).

[3] Downie (1990) contends that the common assumption that professions aim to act in the interest of their clients while those involved in the market are motivated by their own self interest is contentious. He introduces the distinction between tuism and non tuism.

CHAPTER FOUR

SYNTHESIS AND RECOMMENDATIONS

This chapter synthesises the main findings of the literature review. Various recommendations for progressing the idea of professionalism are subsequently reviewed and appraised in the light of these findings. The limitations of the study are highlighted and the chapter concludes with some further areas for research in this field. The following themes are discussed in more detail:

- Conceptualising a response
  - Character and virtue
  - Character and categorisation
  - Intellectual capital, character and competence
  - Ethical knowledge networks

- Practical Recommendations
  - Interdisciplinary perspectives
  - Service Based Learning
  - Pro-Bono Publico

Synthesis

This report has drawn on a broad range of literature to critically explore the ethics of individual accountants. In an attempt to deal with this subject systematically, the title for the study was partitioned into its constituent elements and explored in turn. These issues were:

(i) How does the literature help to conceptualise or model the ethical behaviour of individuals?

(ii) What does it tell us about the ethics of individual accountants in particular?

(iii) What does the literature convey about the nature of professions in general?

(iv) How does this ideal compare with the reality of accounting practice?

(v) What does the literature tell us about the historical development of the accounting profession?

(vi) And finally, what events have and are influencing the way the concept of professionalism is evolving?

Having reviewed the insights the literature provides into each of these issues, this section now summarises and synthesises the main findings.

The literature on the structure of ethical issues and the way that individuals respond to ethics is extensive. This report has identified three broad strands of research that provide insights into individual ethical behaviour. The normative strand explores the traditional moral dilemma of how an individual should act and discusses principle-based and virtue-based responses to this question. The analytical strand focuses on the basis and the nature of ethical claims and focuses attention on the ethical subject's position within a broader community of other individuals. A subsequent key question to arise from this observation is whether or not individual ethical decisions, are or should be, based on reason, or alternatively, some empathetic moral sense. The final strand of research is more empirical in its orientation. This literature suggests that individual attributes can have a significant effect on ethical decision making and highlights the somewhat worrying conclusion that many accountants view accounting as an amoral activity. The literature, however, suggests that this moral illiteracy may only be confined to their role as accountants and that individuals may experience ethical dilemmas in different ways depending on the category, or moral frame within which they are encountered. The implication is that individuals may respond to broadly similar issues in different ways. This broad review of the moral philosophy literature was used to construct a rough working model that might be helpful for beginning to engage with the complexity of the ethics of individual accountants (see Figure 2.2).

The literature on the nature of professionalism is also extensive. This research suggests that traditionally, the idea of professionalism has included, amongst other things: a commitment to the public interest; a coherent body of knowledge supported by a rigorous system of education; independence; and an implied or explicit professional code of conduct. However, within the context of accounting, it has been argued that the profession does not correspond to this ideal type. Some authors have expressed concern that professional accounting education focuses excessively on technical ability. Others are concerned that professional codes of ethics are geared towards protecting the profession and also that they engender rule following, a rather stilted way of approaching ethical dilemmas (Harris and Brown, 1990). Finally, there is significant concern over the nature of the public interest claims of the profession. Of particular worry is the apparent inability of practising accountants to engage with the broader political-economy within which accounting functions. This combination of technical education, ethical rule following and a lack of politico-economic awareness is of particular concern for many commentators. They suggest that these characteristics combine to work against the kind of independent, analytical thinking which is crucial both for engaging with the public interest and progressively developing the civic functioning of accounting within society.

The exploration of both the origin and early composition of the profession suggests that, within accountancy, professionalism may have been loosely related to character and that this in turn may have been influenced by middle-class views of respectability. Early conceptions of the public interest, around the time of the origin of the profession, were articulated in terms of ensuring the technical competence and proper character of those entering the profession. However, as Neu and T'Aerien (2000) suggested, this focus on individual morality, rather than the collective function of the accountancy profession within broader society, represented a very narrow view of the public interest.

Finally, the literature suggests that a number of general and specific changes may have affected professionalism since the profession's initial establishment. Reference is made, at least obliquely, to six general but distinct socio-economic shifts that may have had an impact on individual experiences of professionalism: moral confusion; the demise of trust in authority; changing expectations of business; the increased importance and complexity of business and accounting in general; commercialisation; and finally, advances within the academy.

The model presented in figure 4.1 (see page 77) attempts to capture the salient issues from the literature review. It outlines the descriptive issues that the profession will have to engage with if it is going to begin to understand accountants' existing experiences of professionalism. However, it also presents the profession with a fundamental, normative challenge: based on the analytical moral philosophy literature, how should accountants behave, or more specifically, what should they do? Of course, this is not a question just for the profession. From a democratic, civil-society perspective, this question must be answered by the *demos*, by the broader society that the profession purports to serve, not just the profession or the business community.

However, there is a third component that is, as yet, missing from the model. Once the complexity of the ethics of individual professional accountants has been understood and after it has been established how professionals should behave, consideration needs to be given as to how to make the transition from the prevailing situation towards the ideal. This process of change is complex and the real possibility that any new ideal might end up servicing the *status quo* cannot be fully explored here. However, it is important to stress that any attempt to engage with the changing experiences of professionalism must be marked by requisite complexity. While revised codes of conduct and the regulation of the auditor-client relationship, as per Sarbanes-Oxley, represent important developments, it is questionable whether isolated, un-coordinated and more importantly, un-theorised, responses are likely to substantively change individual accountants perceptions of professional ethics.

Conceptualising a response

Much of the professional debate over how to engage with the ethics of individual accountants is conceptually weak. This is particularly the case when it comes to thinking about engaging in the process of substantive attitudinal change at the individual professional level (see Eiser 1994 for a discussion of attidudinal change). Even within the academic literature, there has been little consideration of how to translate theoretically well-developed notions, like stakeholder theory or social contract theory into the context of the ethical subjectivity, or self-understanding, of the individual professional accountant, despite the fact that such underlying dispositions are crucial to the proper functioning of these notions.

From the literature review above, character emerges as a key concept in the idea of professionalism, whether it is the belief in public service, commitment to the public interest, altruism or a sense of social calling. Also much of the discussion of progress and change within the literature favours the development of some notion of moral character as opposed to a rule-following ethical predisposition (Harris and Brown, 1990; Dillard and Yuthus, 2002). However, how to engage with and develop the moral character of accountants is problematic, given that the historical literature reviewed above contends that it is based on an old, rather nebulous, class-based system that is no longer relevant today.

Drawing loosely on the post-structuralist perspective for orientation[1] (McPhail, 1999), this section tentatively attempts to begin to make a theoretical connection between character, interpreted in terms of ethical subjectivity, and two emerging notions within the literature: intellectual capital and knowledge networks. While this is not the place to develop a detailed theoretical discussion, both these ideas are relatively familiar to the business community and it may, therefore, not be too challenging to envisage how a more detailed model could be developed (see figure 4.1.).

Figure 4.1:Modelling professional ethics - Transition

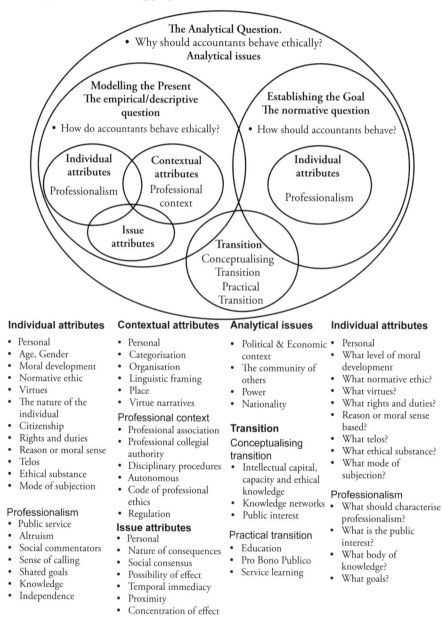

Individual attributes

- Personal
- Age, Gender
- Moral development
- Normative ethic
- Virtues
- The nature of the individual
- Citizenship
- Rights and duties
- Reason or moral sense
- Telos
- Ethical substance
- Mode of subjection

Professionalism
- Public service
- Altruism
- Social commentators
- Sense of calling
- Shared goals
- Knowledge
- Independence

Contextual attributes

- Personal
- Categorisation
- Organisation
- Linguistic framing
- Place
- Virtue narratives

Professional context
- Professional association
- Professional collegial authority
- Disciplinary procedures
- Autonomous
- Code of professional ethics
- Regulation

Issue attributes
- Personal
- Nature of consequences
- Social consensus
- Possibility of effect
- Temporal immediacy
- Proximity
- Concentration of effect

Analytical issues

- Political & Economic context
- The community of others
- Power
- Nationality

Transition

Conceptualising transition
- Intellectual capital, capacity and ethical knowledge
- Knowledge networks
- Public interest

Practical transition
- Education
- Pro Bono Publico
- Service learning

Individual attributes

- Personal
- What level of moral development
- What normative ethic?
- What virtues?
- What rights and duties?
- Reason or moral sense based?
- What telos?
- What ethical substance?
- What mode of subjection?

Professionalism
- What should characterise professionalism?
- What is the public interest?
- What body of knowledge?
- What goals?

The post-structuralist perspective implies that professional, ethical identity is sustained within a nexus of powerful discourse relationships. The following sections begin to explore the links between character and narrative in more detail.

Character and virtue

MacIntyre's work develops a link between ethical subjectivity and narrative where certain characteristics gain their status as virtues from a supporting context. What is regarded as a virtue in one context might not be perceived as such within different historical or cultural settings. In other words, a broader grand narrative sustains the virtues that make up character.

Accounting practice in the West is grounded in the free market, financial utilitarian model which is based on assumptions of values, rights, and duties. However, the literature suggests that accountants generally have quite a poor understanding of the broader social and political function of accounting and little grasp of the specific political economy of accounting practice, but this is only part of the story. There is also a significant volume of literature that critiques the prevailing ethical basis of accounting and presents, what are in principle at least, alternative sources of meaning for the accounting function, which might support different virtues. These alternative perspectives include for example, Social Contract Theory and Stakeholder Theory and view accounting in terms of its broader civic potential.

Although accounting is ultimately based on a comprehensive economic story it operates covertly. This narrative, that is deeply embedded in accounting textbooks and practices, needs to be lifted to the surface and subjected to critical scrutiny by accounting students, practitioners and society in general. If, in the light of this critical analysis, the accounting profession can develop and sustain a more overt broad social narrative, then this may go some way towards promoting a professional subjectivity which has the public interest at its core.

Character and categorisation

The sociology literature discusses whether categorisation is linked to the post-modernist predilection towards the fragmentation of individual consciousness. If it is, then there are certainly implications for the profession's traditional understanding of, and dependence on character. While, historically, an individual may have displayed a common disposition across a number of different roles, post-modern theories suggest that within contemporary society, values and dispositions are more likely to coalesce around particular discourses. If they are correct, then further consideration needs to be given to whether the values that individuals subscribe to in other parts of their lives[2] might be useful in responding to, and engaging with, the development of individual ethical subjectivity.

Intellectual capital, character and competence

A third issue that might potentially be helpful in conceptualising a response to the problem of character can be found in the intellectual capital literature (Power 2001). Peter Drucker, in his book, Post-Capitalist Society, contends that businesses now operate in an economy where the key resource is knowledge. A key argument in the intellectual capital arena is that conventional financial accounting fails to identify key intangible assets and as a consequence fails to convey the real marginal economic value of the company. In an attempt to mitigate against the impact of these reporting weaknesses, some companies have begun to produce Intellectual Capital Statements (Power, 2001; Mouritsen et al. 2001). These reports specify the key competences perceived to be crucial for maintaining companies' continued success. They include things like the knowledge and competence of employees as well as the structural management of knowledge across the institution. Typically, these documents focus on employee competence, internal structure and external structure[3] (Sveiby, 1997).

This literature might be useful for re-conceptualising character within the context of the accounting profession. It is apparent that a knowledge base is one of the defining characteristics of a profession. However, within the accounting profession, the education system seems to be narrowly focused on the technical competence of accountants. The intellectual capital literature opens up the discussion of what is meant by competence and, although not explicitly discussed, it would certainly seem that in the wake of Enron, World Com and Parmalat, ethical and emotional intelligence (McPhail, 2004) must be viewed as a key competence and intangible asset. If the knowledge base of individual accountants constitutes part of the profession's own intellectual capital, and ethical competence is a key component of that asset, then it might stimulate further thinking on the practical and ideological changes which would need to take place to view individual ethical knowledge as a collective structural resource in other words, a resource of the profession. The final section tries to do this by linking intellectual capital with the literature on knowledge networks.

Ethical knowledge networks

The literature on knowledge networks may enable us to construe professional ethical knowledge in a networked, relational sense. Maintaining and embellishing the organisational competence of the profession and its members might, thus, be viewed in terms of networked relationships, as a knowledge network or a knowledge community (Lindkvist, 2003). From this perspective, the experience of ethical dilemmas by practitioners, the tensions associated with these dilemmas, the individual's response and the consequences of a particular mode of behaviour might be viewed as useful pieces of organisational knowledge, or organisational assets. The key is an appreciation of ethical knowledge, in particular, as an organisational resource, how ethical knowledge is generated and what is done with this knowledge. This particular literature may also help in understanding and modelling the various ethical knowledge networks within which the individual accountant is embedded and how ethical knowledge might be transferred and sustained by those networks (Grabher, 2004).

This section has been quite modest in its scope and has simply provided a list of links between emerging concepts in the literature which may be of some help for beginning to conceptualise the development of individual professional subjectivity.

Practical recommendations

This section explores some of the more practical recommendations for progressing the ethical subjectivities of individual accountants which have been considered within the literature. While some of the literature focuses on specific recommendations, it is important to emphasis that no single response can adequately address the complexity of this issue. Indeed, un-theorised, isolated reforms may actually have a harmful impact on professional identity, as in the case of codes of conduct. The review also suggests that any attempt to reinstate some past notion of professionalism would be misplaced. It is clear from the review above that conceptualising the issue simply in terms of trying to make accountants more ethical, more honest and independent, should represent only the beginning of a bigger process of transforming accountants into civic actors, capable of developing their profession in the interests of the public in general, and competent social commentators in matters related to their discipline (Reid, 1980).

While there are many structural and organisational changes which might contribute towards this type of agenda, they are beyond the primary focus of this review. With this in mind, the most pertinent recommendations relating specifically to individual accountants are in the area of education. The literature across the professions consistently argues that education is a key area where a substantive and radical rethink is required. The engineering literature, for example, consistently identifies deficiencies in engineering education as a main contributor to problems within that profession (See Luthy *et al*, 1992). Killingsworth and Twale (1994) imply that engineering education is too technical in nature (See Mickleborough and Wareham, 1994; Florman, 1987; Herkert and Viscomi, 1991; Cassidy *et al.* 1970)[4, 5]. Kucner (1993) comments that students are rarely exposed to the ethics of engineering and Koehn (1991) bemoans the fact that engineers do not have a broad view of the social and ethical implications of their work. Cottell (1993) concludes that 'civil engineers ... must take a much broader view' of what they do[6] (see also Coates, 1993; Koehn, 1991; Lowe, 1991).

Green *et al.* (1995) similarly express concern at evidence which seems to link medical education with diminishing ethical sensitivity amongst medical students and Miles *et al.* (1989) discuss growing concerns that medical education is 'dehumanising doctors' because it focuses primarily on the technical nature of medical practice.

The law literature also suggests that part of the concerns over the ethics of lawyers and the ethical status of the legal profession in general may be related to legal education[7]. Jewell (1984; see also Matasar, 1989) argues that legal education has adopted an unquestioning attitude to ethical issues and Webb (1996) expresses concern that the result of this partial and prejudiced perspective is that law students are oblivious to the ethical dimension of their work. Webb (1996) argues that the law school experience frequently involves students in a process of, 'disillusionment, generating cynicism about legal education and an ethical pragmatism or even amoralism about the lawyer's role in society'.

Yet while there appears to be some general consensus that current modes of professional education in general are deficient, it is also broadly accepted within the literature that substantive educational reforms might represent a potentially effective way of beginning to develop more sophisticated, socially aware, public professionals. There seems to be a considerable degree of consensus within the engineering literature, for example, that the engineering profession could begin to address some of its professional concerns through its system of education (see for example Killingsworth and Twale, 1994; Vesilind, 1991; Koehn, 1991; Koehn and Bourque, 1990; Hauck and Potts, 1990; Tucker, 1983).

Within the law literature, education is identified as a key factor in beginning to address some of the problems of the low ethical characteristics of lawyers. Matasar (1989), for example, argues that some form of ethical discussion should take place in all law school teaching. Similarly, Moliterno (1996) provides some general evidence of the increase in concern for ethics teaching and how to go about it. The Lord Chancellor's Advisory Committee's, the Advisory Committee on Legal Education and Conduct, 'First Report,' also explores the role for legal education in beginning to address problems within the legal profession[8].

Ethics education has also been recognised as an important element in the ethical development of doctors for some time. Ethics has been taught in American medical schools since the 1970s (Gillon 1996) and is now almost universal (Bissonette *et al.* 1995; Grundstein-Amado, 1995; Baylis and Downie, 1991). British medical schools were advised by the General Medical Council to review their *curriculum* and in 1986 the British Medical Association called for all medical schools to include medical ethics in their *curriculum* (Green *et al.* 1995). This recommendation is actually being put into effect and academics are trying to decide what an ethics course would look like (Gillon, 1996). As such, the requirement for ethics education for medical students is almost taken for granted,[9] the question the medical profession is more concerned with is how to go about it (Weatherall, 1995, see also Saunders

1995) and how much more resources to direct towards ethics education in the future (Grundstein-Amado, 1995).

While the literature has indicated that business education may be partially to blame for the ethical problems in the business community, many researchers have also suggested that new forms of education may be used to address these problems (see Gray *et al.* 1994; McPhail, 2001; Patten and Williams, 1990; Lewis *et al.* 1992; Loeb, 1988; The Treadway Commission, 1987; Langenderfer and Rockness, 1989; Loeb and Rockness, 1992; Huss and Patterson, 1993; Hiltebeitel and Jones, 1992; AACSB, 1988; Arlow and Ulrich, 1988; Cohen and Pant, 1989). The National Commission on Fraudulent Financial Reporting in America, for example, noted that ethics education in accounting was at a minimum and recommended the inclusion of ethics in every business and accounting course (Loeb *et al.* 1992; Hiltebeitel and Jones, 1992). Also, The American Assembly of Collegiate Schools of Business (1988, in Hiltebeitel and Jones 1992) suggested that ethics instruction should be included 'in general education courses; in the common body of knowledge; and in the major field of study'. Similarly, Davis and Welton (1991) have contended that 'part of the long-term solution to improving professional ethics is to address the area as it relates to educating future business professionals, *ie.* college students'.

While there seems to be a general argument within the professional literature that education could play a significant part in addressing the low ethical characteristics of professionals, the business ethics literature in particular also contains a debate over the ability of ethics education to affect any change in students ethical tendencies at all (see Rest and Thoma, 1985, in McCabe *et al.* 1991; Hiltebeitel and Jones, 1992; Huss and Patterson, 1993; Goldsman, 1987; Stead and Miller, 1988; Martin, 1981 and Ulrich *et al.* 1993 for a discussion of the positive impacts of ethics education, but see also Weber, 1990; Stead and Miller, 1988; Lane and Shaupp 1989; Rohatyn, 1988; Harris and Brown, 1990; Riemer *et al.* 1983; Boyd, 1987; Forisha and Forisha, 1976, in Davis *et al.* 1991; Borkowski and Ugras,

1992; Wynd and Mager, 1989, in Burton *et al*. 1991). From an analysis of the literature it would appear that this contradictory evidence might be related to two issues. Firstly, methodological problems (Weber 1990), in relation to how the effectiveness of ethics education is measured[10] (see Loeb, 1991; Caplan, 1980; Hiltebeitel and Jones, 1992); and secondly, the way in which ethics is taught (Burton *et al*. 1991). Thus, while there is conflicting evidence, the objective should be to explore those methods of teaching ethics that appear to be having an impact (McPhail, 2001). Indeed these discrepancies reflect a general lack of robust educational theory underpinning many attempts to engage students with the ethics of professional practice.

Despite the many calls for the integration of ethics courses across the professions, there is little evidence, particularly within accounting and business disciplines that programmes have been implemented in any co-ordinated or well structured manner (Cohen and Pant, 1989). Developments in thinking on public interest and accountability are making their way into undergraduate accounting education (Willmott, 1989), and there is evidence of some initial discussion at the professional level (ICAS, 2004). However, these developments seem to be unsystematic and they also tend to be relatively under-theorised from a critical, educational theory perspective. ICAS (2004), for example, in their review of the ethical dispositions of chartered accountants in Scotland conclude with a list of educational reforms. While these reforms are to be welcomed, they need to be viewed as part of a broader programme based on guiding theoretical perspectives. This is true, both in the sense of broad educational goals but also in relation to what ethics education should specifically involve and how it should be taught (McPhail, 2001) and even where it should take place (McPhail, 2002; 2003). For example, the literature reviewed in section two above highlighted a significant debate on whether ethical development should be based on educating the reasoning capabilities of individuals or whether it requires emotional intelligence. If the profession were to introduce compulsory ethical education which model should it be based on?

ICAS's (2004) study does contribute significantly to the debate on ethics education in the profession, however, rather than reiterate some of the material already covered in their report, the remainder of this section attempts to further the discussion by delineating three emerging issues not covered in their study.

Interdisciplinary perspectives

Firstly, it seems from the literature that the dilemmas facing the accounting profession are also being experienced within all of the other major professions. While this may hint at a more generic and endemic crisis in professionalism in general, it also provides an opportunity for engaging with the problem together. As the literature above suggests, not only are the professions experiencing similar problems, all have highlighted education as a potentially important factor in beginning to address these concerns. It would seem that there is scope for a joint, collaborative approach here. Indeed the literature would suggest that bringing students from different disciplines together can engender increased critical awareness of specific, professional, ethical pre-positions. Weisberg and Duffin, (1995) (see also Herndron, 1996) for example provide an account of an ethics course that brought lawyers, doctors and nurses together to explore the ethical conceptions of their professions and the individuals they serve (McPhail, 2001).

Service based learning

A second emerging issue relates to Service Based Learning (SBL) programmes[11]. SBL is an experiential form of education that facilitates student involvement in local community activities in a way that compliments academic studies. Ideally, communities receive assistance and students are given the opportunity to put their education into practice in a project that contributes towards a particular community need. This form of education therefore seeks to advance both academic and civic objectives by combining service with learning (Campus Compact, 2003).

Projects are selected based on their potential to enhance students' understanding of academic issues while engaging them in active citizenship. This engagement generally provides students with the opportunity to critically reflect upon their chosen discipline and the ways in which it can relate to broader civic society. It also conveys to students a particular motivation for learning that challenges what often appears to be a rather strategic and self-interested orientation, at least within the business disciplines. At its core, Service Based Learning seeks to enhance students' 'civic skills' with a view to promoting their engagement within democratic society (Campus Compact, 2003; see also McPhail, 2005).

Pro-Bono Publico

A final issue that might be of some relevance to the development of ethics programmes within the accounting profession is *Pro-Bono Publico*. *Pro-Bono* involves the provision of professional services, normally to those who could not afford them, for free. Although this kind of professional work is more prominent within the legal profession, most of the large accounting firms would support, or at least say they support, some form of *pro-bono* commitment. *Pro-Bono* seems to be more apparent at the institutional level within the legal profession whereas it seems to be undertaken in a less structured way within the accounting profession, primarily through accounting firms. For example, in 1993 the American Bar Association House of Delegates adopted Model Rule 6.1 on Voluntary *Pro-Bono* Public Service, which sets a target of 50 hours per lawyer per year and stipulates that a 'substantial majority' of this commitment must be directed towards people or institutions who could otherwise not afford legal services.

While there are many legitimate concerns within the literature over the reasons why firms become involved in *pro-bono* work, it could potentially provide a vehicle for professional ethical development, provided it is linked to some broader programme of critical education, and perhaps some broader ethical knowledge network (McPhail, 2005).

Further areas for study

While there is a considerable body of diverse research that might be useful for shedding light on the complexity of the ethics of individual professional accountants, bringing this literature together also draws attention to a number of areas that would benefit from further exploration. Four broad gaps can be identified in particular. Firstly, notwithstanding the ICAS (2004) report, there seems to be a lack of research on practicing, professional accountants themselves. Further investigation into practitioners' views of professionalism and how their conceptualisations relate to other value systems to which they subscribe in other areas of their lives might be helpful. Secondly, there is a need for further theoretical work to develop conceptual models for thinking about accounting knowledge and how this relates to professionals' claim to serve the public interest. A recent call for papers for a special edition of *Accounting Auditing and Accountability Journal* on 'Accounting for the Public Interest,' is evidence of a perceived need for further work in this area. There is an extensive literature on accountability and stakeholder models and also Corporate Citizenship and Social Contract Theory (see Lovell (2005), for a more detailed discussion of these developments), however more theoretical work is required on how to translate these ideas into the context of professional knowledge and professional identity. Thirdly, there would seem to be a need for further work on civic education and how notions of the public interest and character might be effectively translated and incorporated into professional education at all levels.

Finally, there is a real need for research in how individuals' perceptions of accounting and what it means to be a professional accountant are developed by their exposure to accounting before attendance at university. While there is a plethora of literature on the attitudes of accounting university students, very little is known about the content and impact of accounting and business education both at the primary and secondary school level. If the profession is to seriously engage with the ethics of individual professionals then it must take a more proactive interest in accounting curriculum development and the promotion of broader, more civic views of business and accounting at these more rudimentary levels.

In the wake of prior crises, the profession has been accused of tokenism (Hauptman and Hill, 1991) and protectionism (Preston *et al.* 1995; Huff and Kelly, 1989; Parker, 1994). It has been criticised for responding in a reactionary manner without fully engaging with the complexities of the nature of ethical issues or the socio-economic context within which they are experienced (Hauptman and Hill, 1991; Preston *et al.* 1995; Parker, 1994). The profession's response to its current crisis is awaited with interest.

Endnotes:

[1] The discussion of the post-structuralist perspective above and the subsequent review of the historical shifts in the nature of professionalism highlight the rather obvious point that both the ideals and the idea of professionalism are social constructs. This perspective also highlights the essentially power-laden context within which any intervention will take place.

[2] For example as Christian, Jew, Muslim, mother, father, environmental consumer and so on.

3   Whereas internal structure includes things like patents, models and computer administrative systems, external structure includes the company's relationship with its customers and also, trademarks and brands.

4   It is contended that real world problems are largely ill defined and much more complex than those presented in engineering degree programmes. Floreman (1987) argues that pure maths and physics taught in isolation does not breed confidence for solving real life engineering problems and that focusing on maths makes students expect one single correct answer. The similarities between this kind of engineering education and accounting education are quite marked.

5   Koehn (1991) notes that there has been growing calls for increased emphasis on the relationship between technology and ethical and social issues.

6   In relation to these issues Tanel (1994) discusses the increased social and political pressures in engineering which are forcing engineers to re-consider the nature of their professional status. Academics are coming to realise the social (Anderson, 1994; Tavakoli, 1992; Coates, 1993) and political (Grigg, 1993) nature of engineering. Grigg (1993) for example highlights the 'highly political' relationship between engineering and a country's infrastructure. As a result the issue of ethics is being articulated in many instances in terms of the engineer's duty to society as a profession. Because engineers are involved in projects which potentially impinge on public health and safety their primary responsibility, it is contested, should be towards society in general (Paschkis, 1975; Anderson, 1994; Holliday, 1994; Tavakoli et al, 1992).

7   Lieberman (1979) argues that the ethical problems in the legal profession may be related to the way the profession was left to develop its own ethical codes of conduct. It is inferred that the codes which were developed benefited the profession more than the public.

8   Webb (1996) argues that this report, for the first time in England, highlighted the importance of addressing ethics within the academic or initial stage of legal education.

9   The pressure for training in medical ethics in general seems to be coming for the increasing complexity of medicine and not a perceived amorality amongst doctors (Hafferty and Franks, 1994 see also Baylis and Downie, 1991).

[10] Weber (1990 in Hiltebeitel and Jones, 1992) suggests that the conflicting results may be due to differences in the sample type; the measurement instrument; the method of analysis and the research focus (for example ethical awareness or ethical reasoning).

[11] While Service Based Learning is beginning to emerge in the UK business literature, these types of programme are fairly well established in the US.

REFERENCES

Abbott, A (1983), "Professional Ethics", *American Journal of Sociology*, pp.855-995.Abbott, A (1988), *System of professions: An essay on the division of expert labour*. Chicago, University of Chicago Press.

Akaah, I P and D Lund (1994), "The influence of personal and organizational values on marketing professionals' ethical behaviour", *Journal of Business Ethics*, 13, pp.417-430.

American Assembly of Collegiate Schools of Business (1988), Accreditation Council Policies, Procedures and Standards, AACSB, St Louis.

American Institute of Certified Public Accountants (1988), *Code Of Professional Conduct*, AICPA, New York.

Anderson J V (1994), "Is it necessary to Compromise Engineering Ethics to Remain Competitive?", *Journal of Professional Issues in Education and Practice*, Vol.120, No.4, July.

Arlow, P (1991), "Personal Chracteristics in College Students' Evaluations of Business Ethics and Corporate Social Responsibility", *Journal of Business Ethics*, 10, pp.63-69.

Arlow P and T A Ulrich (1988), "Can Ethics Be Taught To Business Students", *The Collegiate Forum,* Vol.14, Spring, pp.17.

Armstrong, M B (1987), "Moral Development and Accounting Education", *Journal of Accounting Education,* Vol.5, pp.27-43.

Armstrong, P (1987), 'The Rise of Accounting Controls in British Capitalist Enterprises', *Accounting Organizations and Society*, pp.415-436.

Arthur Anderson & Co, Coopers & Lybrand, Deloitte & Touche, Ernst & Young, KPMG Peat Marwick and Price Waterhouse (1991), *The Public Accounting Profession: Meeting the Needs of a Changing World*, January.

Bachelard, G (1994), *The Poetics of Space*, Beacon Press, Boston.

Backof, J F and C L Martin (1991), "Historical Perspectives: Development of the Codes of Ethics in the Legal, Medical and Accounting Professions", *Journal Of Business Ethics,* 10, pp.99-110.

Baldick, T L (1980), "Ethical Discriminatory Ability of Intern Psychologists: A Function of Training in Ethics", *Professional Psychology,* Vol.11, No.2, pp.276-282.

Bauman, Z (1993), *Postmodern Ethics,* Blackwell, Oxford.

Bauman, Z (1996), *Modernity and The Holocaust,* Blackwell: Oxford.

Bay, D (2002), 'A Critical Evaluation of the use of the DIT in Accounting Ethics Education', *Critical Perspectives on Accounting,* Vol.13(2), pp.159-177.

Bayles, M D (1987), "Professional Power and Self-Regulation", *Business and Professional Ethics Journal,* 5(2), pp.26-46.

Baylis F and J Downie (1991), "Ethics Education for Canadian Medical Students," *Academic Medicine* (66), pp.413-414.

Bebbington, J, I Thomson and D Wall (1997), "Accounting Students and Constructed Gender: An exploration of gender in the context of accounting degree choices", *Journal of Accounting Education,* Vol.15(2), pp.241-267.

Beets, S D and L N Killough (1990), "The Effectiveness of a Complaint-Based Ethics Enforcement System: Evidence from the Accounting Profession", *Journal of Business Ethics,* 9, pp.115-126.

Bissonette, R, R M O'Shea, M Horwitz and C F Route (1995), "A Date-generated Basis for Medical Ethics Education: Categorizing Issues Experienced by Students during Clinical Training", *Academic Medicine,* 70, pp.1035-1037.

Bledstein, B J (1976), *The Culture of Professionalism: The Middle Class and the Development of Higher Education in America,* W W Norton & Co, New York.

Boland, R J Jr. (1982), "Myth and Technology in the American Accounting Profession", *Journal of Management Studies,* Vol.19, No.1, pp.109-127.

Borkowski, S C and Y F Ugras (1992), "The Ethical Attitudes of Students as a Function of Age, Sex and Experience", *Journal of Business Ethics,* Vol.11(12), pp.961-979.

Boyd, C (1987), "The Individualistic Ethic And The Design Of Organisation", *Journal of Business Ethics,* Vol.6, pp.145-151.

Briloff, A J (1990), "Accounting and Society: A Covenant Desecrated", *Critical Perspectives on Accounting,* 1, pp.5-30.

Broadbent, J (1998), "The Gendered Nature of Accounting Logic: Pointers to an Accounting That Encompasses Multiple Values", *Critical Perspectives on Accounting,* 9, pp.267-297.

Brooks L J (1989), "Ethical Codes of conduct: Deficient in Guidance for the Canadian Accounting Profession", *Journal of Business Ethics,* 8, pp.325-335.

Bruce, R (1996), "Whiter than White?", *Accountancy,* May.

Bruneau, M (1994) "Strategies to Enhance Well-Being of Civil Engineering Profession" *Journal of Professional Issues in Education and Practice*, Vol.120, No.4, July.

Bruneau, M. (1993) "Monitoring Well-Being of Civil Engineering Profession " *Journal of Professional Issues in Engineering Education and Practice.* Vol.119, No.1, pp.14-26. Jan.

Burton, S, M W Johnston and E J Wilson (1991), "An Experimentational Assessment of Alternative Teaching Approaches for Introducing Business ethics to Undergraduate Business Students", *Journal of Business Ethics,* Vol.10(7), pp.507-517.

Cambell, D T (1963), *Social Attitudes and Other Acquired Behavioural Dispositions.*

Campus Compact (2003), http://www.compact.org/

Caplan A L (1980), "Evolution and the Teaching of Ethics", in Callahan D and Bok S (eds), *Ethics Teaching In higher Education,* pp.133-150, Plenum Press, New York.

Carey, J L (1970), *The Rise of the Accountancy Profession: To Responsibility and Authority 1937-1969,* AICPA, New York.

Carmichael, D R and R J Swieringa (1968), "The Compatibility of Audit Independence and Management Services – An Identification of Issues", *The Accounting Review*, Oct. pp.697-705.

Carr-Saunders, A M and P A Wilson (1933), *The Professions,* Oxford University Press, Oxford.

Carson, R (1962), *Silent Spring*, Penguin Books, London.

Cassidy, J J, J W Baldwin and A Pauw (1970), "Realistic Civil Engineering Design," *Journal of professional issues in engineering education and practice*, Vol.61(10), pp.130-131.

Choo, F (1989), "Cognitive Scripts in Auditing and Accounting Behavior", *Accounting Organizations and Society*, Vol.14, No.5/6, pp.481-493.

Claypool G A, D F Fetyko and M A Pearson (1990), "Reactions to Ethical Dilemmas: A Study Pertaining to Certified Public Accountants", *Journal of Business Ethics,* 9, pp.699-706.

Clikeman P M, B N Schwartz and M H Lathan (2001), "The Effect of the 150-Hour Requirement on New Accountants' Profesional Commitment, Ethical Orientation and Professionalism", *Critical Perspectives on Accounting,* 12, pp.627-645.

Coates, G H (1993), "Facilitating Sustainable Development : Role of The Engineer" *Journal of Professional Issues in Engineering Education and Practice,* 119(3), July.

Cohen J R, L W Pant and D J Sharp (1992), "Cultural and Socioeconomic Constraints on International Codes of Ethics: Lessons from Accounting", *Journal of Business Ethics,* 11, pp.687-700.

Cohen J R (Ed) (1999), *Educating Minds and Hearts, Social and Emotional Learning and the Passage into Adolescence*, Teachers College Press, New York.

Cohen, J R and L W Pant (1989), "Accounting Educators' Perceptions and Ethics in the Curriculum", *Issues in Accounting Education,* (Spring), pp.70-81.

Cole M and S Scribner (1974), *Culture & Thought: A Psychological Introduction*, Wiley, New York.

Collier, J (1995), "The Virtuous Organization" *Business Ethics, A European Review*, Vol.4, No.3, pp.143-149.

Cooper R W and G L Frank (1997), "Helping Professional in Business Behave Ethically: Why Business Cannot Abdicate It's Responsibility to the Profession", *Journal of Business Ethics,* 16, pp.1495-1466.

Cottell M N T (1993), "Facilitating Sustainable Development: Is Our Approach Correct?", *Journal of Professional Issues in Engineering Education and Practice*, Vol.119, No.3, July.

Craig, J L (1994), "The Business of Public Accounting", *CPA Journal*, 64(8), pp.18-24.

Cullinan, C (2004), "Enron as a symptom of audit process breakdown: can the Sarbanes-Oxley Act cure the disease?", *Critical Perspectives on Accounting*, 15, pp.853-864.

Daly, H E and J B Cobb (1989), *For the Common Good, Redirecting the Economy towards Community, the Environment and a Sustainable Future*, Green Print, London.

David, J M, J Kantor and I Greenberg (1994), "Possible Ethical Issues and Their Impact on the firm: Perceptions Held by Public Accountants", *Journal of Business Ethics,* 13, pp.919-937.

Davis, J R and R E Welton (1991), "Professional Ethics : Business Students' Perception", *Journal of Business Ethics,* 10(6), pp.451-463.

Davis, R R (1984), "Ethical Behavior Re-examined" *Critical Perspectives on Accounting Journal,* Vol.54(12) pp.32-36.

DeMoss, M A and G K McCann (1997), "Without a Care in the World: The Business Ethics Course and Its Exclusion of a Care Perspective", *Journal of Business Ethics*, 16(4), pp.435-443.

Denham R A (1991), (ed) *Ethical Responsibility in Business And The Accounting Profession: Issues, opportunities and education,* University of Alberta.

Dillard J F and K Yuthas (2002), "Ethical Audit Decisions: A Structuration Perspective," *Journal of Business Ethics,* 36, pp.49-64.

Douglas, P C, R A Davidson and B N Schwartz (2001), "The Effect of Organisational Culture and Ethical Orientation on Accountants Ethical Judgement", *Journal of Business Ethics,* 34, pp.101-121.

Downie, R S (1990), "Professions and Professionalism", *Journal of Philosophy of Education,* 24(2), pp.147- 159.

Durkheim, E (1933), The division of labour in society, translated by G Simpson, Collier Macmillan, London.

Dyckman, T R (1974), "Public accounting: guild or profession?" in Sterling R R (Ed), *Institutional Issues in Public Accounting,* Scholars Book Co, Houston, TX.

Edwards, J R (2001), "Accounting Regulation and the Professionalisation Process: An Historical Essay concerning the Significance of P H Abbott", *Critical Perspectives on Accounting,* 12, pp.675-696.

Eiser, J R (1994), *Attitudes Chaos & The Connectionist Mind,* Blackwell, Oxford.

Esland, G (1980), "Professions and Professionalism", in G Esland and G Salaman (Eds.), *The Politics of Work and Occupations,* University of Toronto Press, Toronto.

Everett, J, D Green and D Neu (forthcoming), "Independence, objectivity and the Canadian CA profession", *Critical Perspectives in Accounting.*

Eynon, G, N T Hill and K T Stevens (1997), "Factors that Influence the Moral Reasoning Abilities of Accountants: Implications for Universities and the Profession", *Journal of Business Ethics,* 16, pp.1297-1309.

Fearnley, S and V Beattie (2004), "The Reform of the UK's Auditor Independence Framework after the Enron Collapse: An Example of Evidence-based Policy Making", *International Journal of Auditing,* 8, pp.117-138.

Finegan, J (1994), "The Impact of personal values on judgements of ethical behaviour in the workplace", *Journal of Business Ethics,* 13, pp.747-755.

Fisher, C (1999), "Ethical stances: the perceptions of accountancy and HR specialists of ethical conundrums at work", *Business Ethics: A European Review,* 8(4).

Fiske, S T and S E Taylor (1984), *Social Cognition,* Random House, New York.

Fleming, A I M (1996), "Ethics and accounting education in the UK – a professional approach?", *Accounting Education,* 5(3), pp.207-217.

Florman, S C (1987), *The Civilized Engineer,* St Martin's Press, New York.

Fogarty, T J (1992), "Organisational Socialisation in Accounting Firms: A Theoretical Framework and Agenda for Future Research", *Accounting Organisations and Society,* Vol.17 No.2, pp.129-149.

Fogarty, T J (1995), "Accountant Ethics: A Brief Examination of Neglected Sociological Dimensions", *Journal of Business Ethics,* 14(2), pp.103-115.

Fogarty, T J (1997) "The Education of Accountants in the US. Reason and it's Limits at the Turn of the Century", *Critical Perspectives on Accounting,* 8, pp.45-68.

Forisha, B E and B E Forisha (1976), *Moral Development And Education,* Professional Education Publication, Inc, Lincoln, Nebraska.

Forte, A (2004), 'Business Ethics: A Study of the Moral Reasoning of Selected Business Managers and the Influence of Organizational Ethical Climate', *Journal of Business Ethics,* Vol.51(2), pp.167-173.

Francis, J R (1990), "After Virtue? Accounting as a Moral and Discursive Practice", *Accounting Auditing and Accountability,* Vol.3(3), pp.5-17.

Frankel M S (1989), "Professional Codes: Why, How and with what impact?", *Journal of Business Ethics* 8, pp.109-115.

Fraser, J A (1997), "How many Accountants does it take to change an industry?", Vol.19, No.5, pp.63-69.

Freeman, R E (1984), *Strategic Management: A Stakeholder Approach*, Pitman, Boston.

Friedman, M (1970), "The Social Responsibility of Business is to Increase Profits", *New York Times Magazine*, Sept. 13.

Gaa J (1990), "A Game Theoretic Analysis of Professional Rights and Responsibilities", *Journal of Business Ethics*, 9, pp.159-169.

Gardener, H (1983), *Frames of mind: The Theory of multiple intelligences*, Basic Books, New York.

Gillon, R (1996), "Thinking about a medical school curriculum for medical ethics and law", *Journal of Medical Ethics* 22, pp.323-324.

Goldsman, A H (1987), "Professional Values and the Problem of Regulation", *Business and Professional Ethics Journal*, Vol.5(2), pp.47-59.

Goleman, D (1995), *Emotional Intelligence*, Nantam Books, New York.

Grabher, G (2004), "Learning in Projects, Remembering in Network? Communality, Sociality and Connectivity in Project Ecologies", *European Urban and Regional Studies*, 11(2), pp.103-123.

Gray, R H (2001), "30 years of corporate social accounting, reporting and auditing: what (if anything) have we learnt?", *Business Ethics: a European Review*, 10(1), pp.9-15.

Gray, R H (2002), "Of messiness, systems and sustainability: towards a more social and environmental finance and accounting", *British Accounting Review*, 34(4), pp.357-386.

Gray, R H, J Bebbington and K McPhail (1994), "Teaching Ethics and the Ethics of Teaching: Educating for Immorality and a Possible Case for Social and Environmental Accounting", *Accounting Education*, Vol.3, pp.51-75.

Green B, P D Miller and C P Routh (1995), "Teaching ethics in psychiatry: a one-day workshop for clinical students", *Journal of Medical Ethics,* (21) pp.234-238.

Grenz, S (1997), *The Moral Quest: Foundations of Christian Ethics*, Inter Varsity Press.

Grey, C (1998), "On Being a Professional in a Big Six Firm", *Accounting Organisations and Society,* 23(5/6), pp.569-587.

Grigg, N S (1993), "Infrastructure and economic development: role of civil engineers", *Journal of Professional Issues in Engineering Education and Practice*, Vol. 119, No. 1, pp.51-61.

Grundstein-Amado, R (1995), "Values Education: A new direction for medical education", *Journal of Medical Ethics,* 21, pp.174-178.

Habermas, J (1976), *Legitimation Crisis*, Heinemann, London.

Hacking, I (1994), "The Archeology of Foucault", in *Foucault A Critical Reader*, (ed) Hoy, C D, Blackwell, Oxford.

Hafferty, F W and F Franks (1994), "The Hidden Curriculum, Ethics Teaching and the Structure of Medical Education", *Academic Medicine,* Vol.69, No.11, November.

Hall, R H (1968), "Professionalization and Bureaucratization", *American Sociological Review*, 33, pp.92-104.

Hammond, T (2002), *A White Collar Profession, Africa American certified public accountants since 1921*, University of North Carolina Press.

Hand, S (1997), *The Levinas Reader*, Blackwell, Massachusetts.

Hanlon, G (1994), *The Commercialism of Accountancy – Flexible Accumulation and the transformation of the Service Class*, Macmillan Basingstoke.

Hanlon, G (1996), "Casino Capitalism and the Rise of the Commercialised Service Class – An Examination of the Accountant", Critical Perspectives on Accounting, Vol.7, No.1, pp.339-363.

Harris, C and W Brown (1990), "Developmental constraints on Ethical Behaviour in Business", *Journal of Business Ethics*, 9, pp.855-862.

Hartman, E M (1998), "The Role of Character in Business Ethics", Vol.8(3), pp.547-559.

Hauck, G W and L W Potts (1990), "Bridges: Spanning history and engineering", *Civil Engineering Education. American Society for Engineering Education*, Vol.12(1), pp.1-10.

Hauptman, R and F Hill (1991), "Deride, Abide or Dissent: On the Ethics of Professional Conduct", *Journal of Business Ethics*, 10, pp.37-44.

Hawkins, D I and A B Cocanougher (1972), "Student Evaluations of the Ethics of Marketing Practices: The Role of Marketing Education", *Journal of Marketing*, Vol.36, April, pp.61-64.

Herkert, J R and V B Viscomi (1991), "Introducing Professionalism and Ethics in Engineering Curriculum", *Journal of Professional Issues in Engineering Education and Practice*, Vol.117, No.3 July.

Herndon, N C (1996), "A New Context for Ethics Education Objectives in a College of Business: Ethical Decision-Making Models", *Journal of Business Ethics*, 15, pp.501-510.

Hewstone, M, W Struebe, J Codol and G M Stephenson (1993), *Introduction to Social Psychology*, Blackwell, Oxford.

Hiltebeitel, K M and S.K. Jones (1992), "An Assessment of the Ethics Instruction in Accounting Education", *Journal of Business Ethics*, 11, pp.37-46.

Holliday, M J (1994), "Ethical Responsibilities of Engineering Profession". *Journal of professional issues in engineering education and practice*, Vol.120, No.3, July, p.270.

Hooks, K L (1991), "Professionalism and Self Interest: A Critical View of the Expectations Gap", *Critical Perspectives on Accounting*, Vol.3, pp.109-136.

Hoy, D C (1994), "Power, Repression, Progress: Foucault, Lukes, and The Frankfurt School", In *Foucault A Critical Reader*, (ed) Hoy, C D, Blackwell, Oxford.

Hubbard, T, S O'Callaghan and K Devine (1989), "CPE and the Local Practitioner", *Georgia Journal of Accountancy*, 10, pp.53-63.

Huff, B N and T P Kelly (1989), "Quality Review and You", *Journal of Accountancy*, pp.34-40.

Hughson, R V and P M Kohn (1980), "Ethics", *Chemical Engineering*, Vol.87, No.10 pp.132-147.

Huss, H F and D M Patterson (1993), "Ethics in Accounting: Values Education without Indoctrination", *Journal of Business Ethics,* Vol.12, pp.235-243.

ICAS (2004), *Taking Ethics to Heart*, (eds Helliar, C and J Bebbington), A Discussion Document by the Research Committee of The Institute of Chartered Accountants of Scotland, Edinburgh.

ICAEW (1948), http://www.icaew.co.uk/membershandbook/index.cfm?AUB=tb2i_30160|MNXI_29320, the Institute of Chartered Accountants in England and Wales, London.

Jakubowski, S T, P Chao, S K Huh and S Maheshwari (2002), 'A cross-country comparison of the codes of professional conduct of certified/ chartered accountants', *Journal of Business Ethics*, 35, pp.111-129.

Jamal, K and N E Bowie (1995), "Theoretical Considerations for a Meaningful Code of Professional Ethics", *Journal of Business Ethics,*14, pp.703-714.

Jeffrey, C (1993), "Ethical Development of Accounting Students, Non-Accounting Business Students and Liberal Arts Students", *Issues in Accounting Education*, 8(1), pp.86-96.

Jensen, L C and S A Wygant (1990), "The Developmental Self-Valuing theory: a Practical approach for Business Ethics", *Journal of Business Ethics,* 9, pp.215-225.

Jewell, M (1984), "Teaching Law Ethically: is it Possible?", *Dalhousie Law Journal*, 8, p.474.

Johnson, T (1982), "The State and the professions: peculiarities of the British", in Giddens, A & MacKenzie, G (Eds), *Social class and the division of labour,* Cambridge University Press, Cambridge.

Jones, T M (1991), "Ethical Decision Making by Individuals in Organisations: An Issue-Contingent Model", *Academy of Management Review,* 16(2), pp.366-395.

Karnes, A, J Sterner, R Welker and F Wu (1990), "A Bi-cultural comparison of Accountants Perceptions of Unethical Business Practices", *Accounting Auditing and Accountability Journal,* 3(3), pp.45-62.

Kedslie, M J M (1990), "Mutual Self Interest- A Unifying Force; the Dominance of Societal Closure Over Social Background in the Early Professional Accounting Bodies", *The Accounting Historians Journal,* 17(2), pp.1-19.

Kerr, S, M A Von Glinow and J Schriesheim (1977), "Issues in the Study of Professionals in Organisations: The Case of Scientists and Engineers", *Organizational Behaviour and Human Performance,* pp.329-345.

Killingsworth, R A and D J Twale (1994), "Integrating Ethics into Technical Curricula", *Journal of professional issues in engineering education and practice,* Vol.120, No.1, January, pp.58-69.

Kirkham, L M and A Loft (1993), "Gender and the Construction of the Professional Accountant", *Accounting Organisations and Society,* 18(6), pp.507-558.

Koehn, E and J Bourque (1990), "Professionalism, ethics and image of civil engineers", *Education and Continuing Development for the Civil Engineer: Setting the Agenda for the 1990's and Beyond ASCE,* pp.968-974.

Koehn, E (1991), "An Ethics and Professionalism Seminar in the Civil Engineering Curriculum", *Journal of professional issues in engineering education and practice,* Vol.117, No.2, April, p.96.

Koehn, E (1992), "Practitioner Involvement with Engineering Ethics and Professionalism", *Journal of professional issues in engineering education and practice,* Vol.118, No.1, January, pp. 49-55.

Kracher, B, A Chatterjee and A R Lundquist (2002), "Factors Related to the Cognitive Moral Development of Business Students and Business Professionals in India and the United States: Nationality, Education, Sex and Gender", *Journal of Business Ethics*, Vol.35, pp.255-268.

Kronman, A (1993), *The Last Lawyer,* Belknap Press, Cambridge, Ma.

Kucner, L K (1993), "Professional Ethics Training for Engineering Firms", *Journal of professional issues in engineering education and practice,* Vol.119, No.2, April, pp.170-181.

Lane, M S (1988), "Pygmalion Effect: An Issue for Business Education & Ethics", *Journal of Business Ethics*, Vol.7, pp.223-229.

Lane, M S and D Shaupp (1989), "Ethics in Education: A Comparative Study", *Journal of Business Ethics,* Vol.8(1), pp.943-949.

Langenderfer, H Q (1987), "Accounting Education's History: A 100-year search for identity", *Journal of Accountancy*, (3), pp.316-329.

Langenderfer, H Q and J W Rockness (1989), "Integrating Ethics into Accounting Curriculum: Issues, Problems and Solutions', *Issues in Accounting Education,* Vol.4, pp.58-69.

Larson, M S (1977), T*he Rise of Professionalism: A Sociological Analysis,* University of California Press, Berkeley.

Lee, T (1995), "The Professionalisation of Accountancy: A History of Protecting Public Interest in a Self-interested Way", *Accounting Auditing and Accountability Journal,* 8(4), pp.48-69.

Lehman C R (1988), "Accounting Ethics: Surviving Survival of The Fittest", *Advances in Public Interest Accounting*, 2, pp.71-82.

Lewis, L, C Humphery and D Owen (1992), "Accounting and the Social: A Pedagogic Perspective", *British Accounting Review*, Vol.24,No.3, September.

Libby, T and L Thorne (2004), "The identification and characterization of auditors virtues", *Business Ethics Quarterly,* Vol.14(3), pp.479-498.

Lieberman, J K (1979), "Moral Choices: Ethics and Values in the 80's Putting Law into Ethics", *Liberal Education*, Vol.65, No.2, pp.259-265.

Likierman, A (1989), "Ethical Dilemmas for Accountants: A United Kingdom Perspective", *Journal of Business Ethics*, 8, pp.617-629.

Lindkvist, L (2003), "Knowledge Communities and Knowledge Collectivities. Different Notions of Group Level Epistemology", paper presented at the 19th EGOS Colloquium, Copenhagen.

Loeb, S E (1988), "Teaching Students Accounting Ethics: Some Critical Issues", *Issues In Accounting Education*, Fall, pp.316-329.

Loeb, S E (1991), "The Evaluation of Outcomes of Accounting Ethics Education", *Journal of Business Ethics*, Vol.10(2), pp77-84.

Loeb, S E and J Rockness (1992), "Accounting Ethics and Education: A Perspective", *Journal of Business Ethics*, Vol.11(7), pp.485-490.

Lovell, A (2005), *Ethics in Business: A Literature Review,* The Institute of Chartered Accountants of Scotland.

Lowe, J G (1991), "Interdisciplinary Postgraduate Education for Construction Managers", *Journal of Professional Issues in Engineering Education and Practice*, Vol.117, No.2, pp.168, April.

Luban, D (ed) (1983), *The Good Lawyer: Lawyers' Roles and Lawyers' Ethics*, Rowan & Allanheld, Totowa.

Luthy, R G, D A Bella, J R Hunt, H Johnson, D F Lawler, D R O'Melia and F G Pohland (1992), "Future Concerns in Environmental Engineering Graduate Education", *Journal of Professional Issues in Engineering Education and Practice*, Vol.118, No.4, October, pp.361-380.

Lysonski, S and W Gaidis (1991), "A Cross-Cultural Comparison of the Ethics of Business Students", *Journal of Business Ethics,* 10, pp.141-150.

McCabe, D L, J M Dukerich and J E Duttin (1991), "Context, Values and Moral Dilemmas: Comparing the Choices of Business Students and Law School Students", *Journal of Business Ethics,* Vol.10(12), pp.951-960.

Macdonald, K M (1984), "Professional Formation: The Case of Scottish Accountants", *The British Journal of Sociology*, 80(2).

MacIntyre, A (1998), *A Short History Of Ethics A History Of Moral Philosophy From The Homeric Age To The Twentieth Century*, 2nd Edition, Routledge & Kegan Paul, London.

MacIntyre, A (1982), *After Virtue: A Study in Moral theory*, Duckworth, London.

Mackie, J L (1977), *Ethics: Inventing Right and Wrong,* Penguin, Harmondsworth.

McDonald, M (1992), "The Canadian Research Strategy for Applied Ethics: a New Opportunity for Research in Business and Professional Ethics", *Journal of Business Ethics,* Vol.11, pp.569-583.

McKernan, J and P O'Donnell (1997), "Financial Accounting: Crisis and the Commodity Fetish", *Critical Perspectives on Accounting*, Vol.9(5), pp.567-599.

McNaughton, D (1988), *Moral Vision an Introduction to Ethics*, Basil Blackwell, Oxford.

McPhail, K J (1999), "The Threat of Ethical Accountants: An Application of Foucault's Concept of Ethics to Accounting Education and Some Thoughts on Ethically Educating for the Other", *Critical Perspectives on Accounting,* Vol.10, pp.833-866.

McPhail K J (2001), "The Other Objective of Ethics Education: Re-humanising the Accounting Profession – A Study of Ethics Education in Law, Engineering, Medicine and Accounting", *Journal of Business Ethics*, Vol.34, pp.279-298.

McPhail, K J (2002), "Using Porridge to Teach Business Ethics: Reflections on a Visit to Scotland's most Notorious Prison and Some Thoughts on the Importance of Location in Teaching Business Ethics", *Journal of Teaching Business Ethics*, 6/3, pp.355-369.

McPhail, K J (2003), "Relocating Accounting & Business Ethics: Reflections on a Business Ethics Retreat in Scotland's National Park", *British Accounting Review*, 35(4), pp.367-384.

McPhail, K J (2004), "An Emotional Response to the State of Accounting Education: Developing Accounting Students' Emotional Intelligence", *Critical Perspectives on Accounting*, Vol.15(4-5), pp.629-648.

McPhail, K J (2005), 'Care in the Community: Professional Ethics & The Paradox of *Pro-Bono*', *Accounting Education*, Vol.14(2), pp.213-227.

Macklin, R (1980), "Problems in Teaching of Ethics: Pluralism and Indoctrination", *Ethics in Higher Education*, pp.61-101, Plenum Press, New York.

Magnet, M (1986), "The Decline and Fall of Business Ethics", *Fortune*, December, pp.65-72.

Markus, H (1977), "Self-schemata and Processing Information about the Self", *Journal of Personality & Psychology*, Vol.35, pp. 63-78.

Martin, M W and R Schinzinger (1989), *Ethics in Education*, 2nd Ed. McGraw-Hill Book Co. New York.

Martin, T R (1981), "Do Courses in Ethics Improve the Ethical Judgement of students?", *Business and Society*, Vol.20 No.2, pp.17-26.

Matasar, R A (1989), "Teaching Ethics in Civil Procedure Courses" *Journal of Legal Education*, Vol.39, No.4, pp.587-607.

Mayer, J (1988), "Themes of social Responsibility: A Survey of Three Professional Schools", *Journal of Business Ethics*, 7(4), pp.313-320.

Merritt, S (1991), "Marketing Ethics and Education: Some Empirical Findings", *Journal Of Business Ethics*, Vol.10, pp.623-632.

Mickleborough, N C and D G Wareham (1994), "Teaching Engineering to Increase Motivation", *Journal of Professional Issues In Engineering Education and Practice*, Vol.120(1), pp.29-35.

Miesing, P and J F Preble (1985), "A comparison of five business philosophies", *Journal of Business Ethics*, Vol.(4), pp.465-476.

Miles, S H, L W Lane, J Bickle, R M Walker and C K Cassel (1989), "Medical Ethics Education: Coming of Age", *Academic Medicine*, (64), December, pp.705-714.

Millerson, G (1964), *The Qualifying Associations*, Routledge and Kegan Paul, London.

Mitchell, A and P Sikka (1993), "Accounting for Change: the Institutions of Accountancy", *Critical Perspectives on Accounting*, 4, pp.29-52.

Mitchell, A, P Sikka and H Willmott (1998), "Sweeping it under the Carpet: The role of Accountancy Firms in Moneylaundering", *Accounting Organizations and Accountancy*, Vol.23(5/6), pp.589-607.

Modic, S J (1987), "Corporate Ethics: From Commandments to Commandment", *Industry Week*, December, pp.33-36.

Moliterno, J E (1996), "On The Future of Integration Between Skills and Ethics Teaching: Clinical Legal Education in the Year 2010", *Journal of Legal Education*, Vol.46 No.1.

Moore, J F and M J R Gaffikin (1994), "The early growth of corporations leading to the empowerment of the accounting profession 1600-1855", *Accounting History*, 6(2), pp.46-65.

Morrison, M A (2004), "Rush to Judgement: The lynching of Arthur Andersen & Co." *Critical Perspectives on Accounting*, 15, pp.335-375.

Mouritsen, J, H T Larsen and P N D Bukh (2001), "Intellectual capital and the 'capable firm': narrating, visualising and numbering for managing knowledge", *Accounting Organizations and Society*, 26, pp.735-762.

Myser, C, I H Kerridge and K R Mitchell (1995), "Teaching clinical ethics as a professional skill: bridging the gap between knowledge about ethics and its use in clinical practice", *Journal of Medical Ethics*, Vol.21, pp.97-103.

Nassuti, C P (1994), "Four Case Studies in Marketing", *Journal of Accountancy*, Vol.178(2), pp.51-56.

Neu, D and R T'Aerien (2000), "Remembering the Past: Ethics and The Canadian Chartered Accounting Profession, 1911-1925", *Critical Perspectives on Accounting*, Vol.11, pp.193-212.

Nielsen, R P (1991), "I Am We Consciousness and Dialog as Organizational Ethics Method", *Journal of Business Ethics*, 10, pp.649-663.

Norris, D R and R E Niebuhr (1983), "Professionalism, Organisational Commitment and Job Satisfaction in an Accounting Organisation", *Accounting Organizations and Society*, Vol.(1), pp.49-59.

Parker, M (1995), "Autonomy, problem-based learning and the teaching of medical ethics", *Journal of Medical Ethics*, Vol.21, pp.305-310.

Parker, L D (1994), "Professional Accounting Body Ethics: In Search of the Private Interest", *Accounting Organisations and Society*, Vol.19(6), pp.507-525.

Parsons, T (1954), *Essay in Sociological Theory*, Collier-Macmillan, London.

Paschkis, V (1975), "Preface", Conference on Engineering Ethics, ASCE, New York NY.

Patten, R J and D Z Williams (1990), "There's Trouble-Right Here in our Accounting Programs: The Challenge to Accounting Educators", *Issues in Accounting Education*, Vol.5(2), pp.175-179.

Pierce, A (2006), *Ethics and the Professional Accounting Firm*, The Institute of Chartered Accountants of Scotland, Edinburgh.

Ponemon, L A (1992), "Ethical Reasoning and Selection-Socialization in Accounting", *Accounting Organizations and Society,* Vol.17(3/4), pp.239-258.

Ponemon, L A (1990), "Ethical Judgements in Accounting: A Cognitive -Development Perspective", *Critical Perspectives on Accounting*, Vol.1(2), pp.191-215.

Porter, J C (1993), "Ethics in Practice", *Journal of Professional Issues in Engineering Education and Practice*, Vol.119, No.1, Jan.

Power, M (2001), "Imagining, measuring and managing intangibles", *Accounting Organisations and Society*, Vol.26, pp.691-693.

Power, M (1992), "The Politics of Brand Accounting in the United Kingdom", *European Accounting Review*, Summer, pp.30-68.

Preston A M, D J Cooper, D P Scarbrough and R C Chilton (1995), "Changes in the Code of Ethics of the US Accounting Profession, 1917 and 1988: the Continual Quest for Legitimation", *Accounting Organisations and Society*, 20(6), pp.507-546.

Previts, G J and D D Merino (1979), *A History of Accounting in America: A Historical Interpretation of the Cultural Significance of Accounting*, Ronald Press, New York.

Puxty, A G (1997), "Accounting Choice and a Theory of Crisis: The Cases of Post-Privatization British Telecom and British Gas", *Accounting Organizations and Society*, Vol.22 No.7, pp.713-735.

Radcliffe, V S, D J Cooper and K Robson (1994), "The Management of Professional Enterprises and Regulatory Change: British Accountancy and the Financial Services Act, 1986", *Accounting, Organizations and Society*, Vol.19, pp.601-628.

Reid, J Y (1980), *Higher Education's Cultural Obligations: Views and Reviews*, ERIC ED 1B5 B79.

Reiter, S A (1996), "The Kohlberg-Gilligan Controversy: Lessons for Accounting Ethics Education", *Critical Perspectives on Accounting*, Vol.7 pp.33-54.

Rest, J (1983), "Morality" in P Mussen (Ed) *Manual of Child Psychology*, pp.556-629, Wiley, New York.

Rest, J and S J Thoma (1985), "Relation of Moral Judgement and Development to Formal Education', *Developmental Psychologist*, Vol.21, pp.709-714.

Richards, D G (1984), "The Future of the Profession", J. Shaw (Ed.), *Contemporary Issues in Accounting*, Pitman, London.

Riemer, J, D Paolitto and R Hersh (1983), *Promoting Moral Growth: From Piaget to Kholberg*, New York, Longman Inc.

Roberts, R W (2001), "Commercialism and it's Impact on the Integrity of Professional Tax Services in the United States", *Critical Perspectives on Accounting*, 12, pp.589-605.

Rohatyn, F G (1988), "Ethics in American Money Culture" in *Ethics in American Business: A Special Report*, Touche Ross, New York.

Rosen, B and A L Caplan (1990), "Ethics in the Undergraduate Curriculum", *The Teaching of Ethics*, Institute of Society, Ethics and Life Sciences, New York.

Ruland, R G and C K Lindblom (1992), "Ethics and disclosure: an Analysis of conflicting Duties", *Critical Perspectives on Accounting*, 3, pp.259-272.

Saunders, M (1995), "The Forgotten Curriculum: An argument for medical ethics education", *Journal of The American Medical Association*, Vol.274, pp.768-769.

Schlachter, .J (1990), "Organisational Influences on Individual Ethical Behaviour in Public Accounting," *Journal of Business Ethics*, 9, pp.839-853.

Schulte, A A (1966), "Management Services: A Challenge to Audit Independence?," *The Accounting Review*, October, pp.721-728.

Schultz, J J (Ed) (1989), *Reorienting Accounting Education: Reports on the Environment, Professoriate, and Curriculum of Accounting*, American Accounting Association, Vol.10.

Serwenek, P J (1992), "Demographic & Related Differences in Ethical Views Among Small Businesses", *Journal of Business Ethics*, Vol.11(7), pp.555-566.

Shackleton, K (1999), "Gender segregation in Scottish chartered accountancy: the deployment of male concerns about the admission of women 1900-25", *Accounting, Business & Financial History*, 9(1), pp.135-156.

Shafer, W E, R E Morris and A A Ketchland (2001), "Effects of Personal Values on Auditors Ethical Decisions", *Accounting Auditing and Accountability Journal*, pp.254-277.

Shaw, B (1997), "Sources of Virtue: The Market and the Community", *Business Ethics Quarterly*, Vol.7(1), pp.33-50.

Shaw, M E and J M Wright (1967), *Scales for the Measurement of Attitudes*, McGraw Hill, New York.

Sikka, P and H Willmott (1995), "The power of 'independence': defending and extending the jurisdiction of accounting in the United Kingdom", *Accounting Organisations and Society*, 20(6), pp.547-581.

Sikka, P, H Wilmott and A Lowe (1989), "Guardians of knowledge and public interest: evidence and issues of accountability in the UK accounting profession", *Accounting, Auditing and Accountability Journal*, 2(2), pp.47-71.

Sims, R R (1992), "Linking Groupthink to Unethical Behavior in Organizations", *Journal of Business Ethics*, 11 pp.651-662.

Smith, M B E (1990), "Should Lawyers Listen to Philosophers about Legal Ethics?", *Law and Philosophy*, 9, pp.67-93.

Spranger, E (1928), *Types of Men*, Max Niemeyer Veriag, Halle Saale, Germany.

Stahlberg, D and D Frey (1988), *Angewandle Psychologie: ein Lehebuch*, Psycologi Verlags Union, Munchen.

Stanga, K G and R A Turpen (1991), "Ethical Judgements on Selected Accounting Issues: An Empirical Study", *Journal of Business Ethics*, 10, pp.739-747.

Stead, B A and J J Miller (1988), "Can Social Awareness Be Increased Through Business Curricula?", *Journal of Business Ethics*, 7(7), pp.553-560.

Sundem, G L (1989), *The Accounting Education Change Commission: It's History and Impact*, Accounting Education Change Commission and American Accounting Association.

Sveiby, K E (1997), *The new organizational wealth: Managing and measuring knowledge based assets*, Berrett-Koehler, San Francisco.

Tajfel, H and C Fraser (1990), *Introducing Social Psychology* Penguin Books, Harmondsworth.

Tanel, B (1994), "Outlook for Environmental Education in 21st Century", *Journal of Professional Issues in Engineering, Education and Practice*, Vol.120(1), January.

Tavakoli, A, R G Ashmum and C S Collyard (1992), "Socio-economic Accounting in Construction", *Journal of Professional Issues in Engineering Education and Practice*, Vol.118, No.2, April.

Taylor, S E and J Corcker (1981), "Schematic Bases of Social Information Processing", in Higgins, E T, C P Herman and M P Zanna (eds), *Social Cognition, The Ontario Symposium*, Vol.1, pp. 89-134, Lawrence Erlbaum Associate, Hillsdale N.J.

Thurow, L (1987), "Ethics Doesn't Start In Business Schools", *New York Times*, June 14, pp.E25.

Tinker, T (1984), "Theories of the State and the State of Accounting: Economic Reductionism and Political Voluntarism in Accounting Deregulation Theory", *Journal of Accounting and Public Policy*, 3(1), pp.55-74.

Touch Ross & Co. (1988), *"Ethics In American Business : A Special Report"*, Touche Ross & Co, New York.

The Treadway Commission (1987), *Report of the National Commission on Fraudulent Financial Reporting*, AICPA, New York.

Trevino, L K (1992), "Moral Reasoning and Business Ethics: Implications for Research, Education and Management", *Journal of Business Ethics*, Vol.11, pp.445-459.

Tucker, W H (1983), "Dilemma in teaching engineering ethics", *Journal of Chemical Engineering Process*, Vol.79(4), pp.20-25.

Tyson, T (1990), "Believing that Everyone Else is Less Ethical: Implications for Work Behaviour and Ethics Instruction", *Journal of Business Ethics*, 9, pp.715-721

Ulrich, P and U Thielemann (1993), "How Do Managers think About Market Economies and Morality? Empirical Inquiries into

Business-ethical Thinking Patterns", *Journal of Business Ethics,* Vol.12, pp.879-898.

Unerman, J and B O'Dwyer (2004), "Enron, WorldCom, Andersen *et al.*: a challenge to modernity", *Critical Perspectives on Accounting,* 15, pp.971-993.

Van Luijk, H J L (1990), "Recent Developments in European Business Ethics", *Journal of Business Ethics,* 9, pp.537-544.

Vann, W P (1992), "Engineering Ethics Bibliography", Ethics workshop, Murdough Centre for Engineering Professionalism, Austin, Texas.

Velayutham, S (2003), "The Accounting Professions Code of Ethics: Is it a code of ethics or a code of quality assurance?", *Critical Perspectives on Accounting,* 14, pp.483-503.

Vesilind, P A (1991), "Views on Teaching Ethics and Morals", *Professional Issues in Engineering Education And Practice,* Vol.117, No.2, April.

Walker, S P (1988), "The Society of Accountants in Edinburgh 1854-1914", *A Study of Recruitment to a New Profession,* Garland Publishing, New York.

Walker, S P (1991), "The Defence of Professional Monopoly: Scottish Chartered Accountants" and "Satellites in the Accounting Firmament 1854-1914", *Accounting Organisations and Society,* 16(3), pp.257-283.

Walker, S P (1995), "The genesis of professional organisation in Scotland: a contextual analysis", *Accounting, Organizations and Society,* 20(4), pp.285-310.

Walker, S P (2004a), "The genesis of professional organisation in English accountancy", *Accounting, Organizations and Society,* 29(2), pp.127-156.

Walker, S P (2004b), "The emergence and consolidation of the profession of chartered accountancy in Scotland", in R Bruce (ed), *ICAS: 150 Years and Still Counting,* ICAS, Edinburgh, pp.15-37.

Walker, S P (1996), "The criminal upperworld and the emergence of a disciplinary code in the early chartered accountancy profession", *Accounting History*, 1(2), pp.7-35.

Waples, E and M K Shaub (1991), "Establishing an Ethic of Accounting: A Response to Westra's Call for Government Employment of Auditors", *Journal of Business Ethics*, Vol.10(5), pp.385-393.

Wasserstrom, R (1984), "Legal Education and the Good Lawyer", *Journal of Legal Education*, June, 34(2), pp.155-162.

Webb, J (1996), "Inventing the Good: A Prospectus For Clinical Education and the Teaching of Legal Ethics in England", *The Law Teacher*, Vol.30(3), pp.270-294.

Weber, J (1990), "Measuring the impact of Teaching Ethics to Future Managers: A Review, Assessment and Recommendations", *Journal of Business Ethics*, Vol.9(3), pp.183-190.

Westra, L (1986), "Whose 'Loyal Agent'? Towards an Ethic of Accounting", *Journal of Business Ethics*, 5, pp.119-128.

West, B (1996), "The Professionalisation of accounting: A Review of recent historical research and its implications", *Accounting History*, pp.77-102.

Weatherall, D J (1995), "Teaching ethics to medical students", *Journal of Medical Ethics*, Vol.21, pp.133-134.

Weisberg M and J Duffin (1995), "Evoking the Moral Imagination: Using Stories to Teach Ethics and Professionalism to Nursing, Medical and Law Students", *The Journal of Medical Humanities*, 16(4), pp.247-262.

Whetsone, J T (2001), "How Virtue Fits Within Business Ethics", *Journal of Business Ethics*, Vol.33, pp.101-114.

Whipple, T W and F F Swords (1992), "Business Ethics Judgements: a Cross-Cultural Comparison", *Journal of Business Ethics*, 11, pp.671-678.

Wilcox, J R (1983), "The teaching of engineering ethics," *Journal of Chemical Engineering Process*, Vol.79(5), pp.15-20.

Williams, P (2004), "Recovering accounting as a worthy endeavour", *Critical Perspectives on Accounting*, 15, pp.513-517.

Williamson, B (1996), "Medical Ethics, teaching and the new genetics", *Journal of Medical Ethics*, Vol.22, pp.325-326.

Williams, J R, H Herring, M Tiller and J Scheiner (1988), *A Framework for the Development of Accounting Education Research*, American Accounting Association Vol.9.

Willmott, H (1986), "Organizing the Profession: A Theoretical and Historical Examination of the Development of the Major Accountancy Bodies in the UK", *Accounting Organizations and Society*, 22(8), pp.831-842.

Willmott, H C (1989), "Serving The Public Interest? A Critical Analysis of a Professional Claim" in Cooper, D J and T M Hooper (eds), *Critical Accounts*, pp.315-331, MacMillan, Basingstoke.

Willmott, H and P Sikka (1997), "On the Commercialization of accountancy thesis: a review essay", *Accounting Organizations & Society*, 22(8), pp.831-842.

Wynd, W R and J Mager (1989), "The Business And Society Course: Does It Change Students Attitudes?", *Journal of Business Ethics*, Vol.8, pp.487-491.

Zeff, S A (1989), "Recent Trends in Accounting Education and Research in the USA: Some Implications for UK Academics", *The British Accounting Review*, 21(2), pp.159-176.

Zeff, S A (1987), "Does the CPA Belong to a Profession?", *Accounting Horizons*, 1(2), pp.65-68.

APPENDIX ONE

This appendix provides a list of the resources specifically covered by the literature review.

Database Search Engines

- OCLC First Search

Accounting and Business Ethics Journals

- Accounting, Auditing & Accountability
- Accounting, Organizations & Society
- Business Ethics: A European Review
- Critical Perspectives on Accounting
- The Journal of Business Ethics

Other Professional Journals

- Journal of Professional Issues in Engineering Education and Practice
- Journal of Medical Ethics.